SUPER IMMUNITY SECRETS

by Cary Ellis

Learn to make the recipes in this book and use the powerful Super Immunity Ingredients and you will have a repertoire of healthy meals that will never fail you.

http://www.caryellis.com

Get Healthy Now Productions
Virtual Earth Village Publishing

PO Box 2652, Springs, Colorado 81147

Dedication and Disclaimer

In our complex modern world, we've almost forgotten that when living in harmony with nature, wellness is often the result… This book is dedicated to those seeking to learn about natural ways of living that include whole foods and simple dietary practices, proven in clinical studies to be effective against viruses, bacteria, cancer and other degenerative illness.

This is a book about how to shop for, prepare and enjoy foods demonstrated by scientific research to have protective qualities. It is neither a prescription nor intended to replace the advice of physician or qualified health professional whose advice should be sought before implementing dietary, prescriptive or lifestyle changes.

This information is provided as is, and by purchasing the book, ebook, videos or using the associated website, the reader agrees to take full responsibility for use of the material herein contained. Seek the assistance of a physician or qualified health professional before making any dietary or lifestyle changes.

Super Immunity Secrets

This edition published by Virtual Earth Village Publishing
cary@virtualearthvillage.com

Virtual Earth Village Publishing
P.O. Box 2652
Pagosa Springs, Colorado 81147

ISBN 978-0-9841711-0-1

KEYWORDS: immune system, easy vegetarian meals, vegetarian soup, immune system support, getting rid of colds and flu, swine flu, natural cold remedies, cold relief, cold prevent, vegetarian diets, vegan diet, veggie recipes, healthy diet, healthy food, healthy vegetarian diet, vegan meals, vegan vegetarian recipes, nutrition vegetarian diet, vegan food diet, healthy quick recipes, natural cold remedy, easy recipes vegetarian, natural immune support, cures cold, what vegetarians eat, how to get rid of flu, cold home remedies, herbal cold remedies, colds prevent, home remedies flu, colds cure, immune system vitamins, immune system diet

Library of Congress Control Number: _____

Acknowledgement

Standing on the shoulders of giants, I am thankful to many health pioneers of the 19th and 20th centuries whose wisdom seeded my learning and growth in this field; and to the *ancients* who lived with an everyday understanding of herbs, spices and foods for healing, longevity and well-being.

Through many years of working with those recovering health I've learned that the body's true energy is towards wellness and what we have to learn is how to get out of its way.

I deeply appreciate the *many* wonderful friends and family (you know who you are) who've supported, had faith in my work and cheered me on over the years.

And of course, I'm so appreciative to my partner Randall whose presence in my daily life gives me courage and sustenance to keep on with my visions and dreams. *Thank you all!*

CONTENTS

Chapter 1: Introduction

WHAT ARE SUPER IMMUNITY SECRETS?

How well we resist viruses, bacteria, colds and flu, and even cancer, arthritis, heart disease and other degenerative conditions **has to do with** *how we live EVERYDAY.*

When sickness appears, we often wonder how to get **better.** Yet as the old saying goes, *an ounce of prevention is worth a pound of cure.* Once sick, common solutions such as drugs mask symptoms, but don't make us well. Wellness is a lifestyle!

A strong vital Immune System and Being Well or knowing how to recover easily results from Daily Habits. This book is filled with *how to's* of a *wellness lifestyle.*

SUPER IMMUNITY LIFESTYLE HABITS:
- ❖ Lighter Diet Cleanse Nourish Cells
- ❖ Optimum Nutritional Practices:
  - Salads, veggies, sprouts, fruits, moderate whole grains, beans
  - At least 50% raw/live foods
  - Reduce/eliminate packaged processed "dead" foods
  - Reduce animal foods max 7%
  - Organic/local foods
  - Include 10% "superfoods"
- ❖ Periodic Cleanse fiber, juices, herbs
- ❖ Be Active, Walk, Work Out
- ❖ Sunshine, Fresh Air, Touch Earth
- ❖ Rest. Less Stress, Spiritual Connect
- ❖ Love Self & Others
- ❖ Creative Mind, Envision, Intend
  - Renew, Regenerate, Affirm Lean Fit Body

MISSION OF THIS BOOK

This information is designed to help you incorporate a more protective lifestyle. Our delicious recipes are made from familiar foods found in your local market or natural food store; no costly exotic things from far away - just real basics to fit into everyday life. Our goal is to help you discover and enjoy healthier tastes!

These recipes, menus and tips are simple, delicious and good; quick and easy to prepare for anyone: single parent, retiree, young person, individual or family on a budget!

WHAT IS DIETARY TRANSITION?

Do we have to give something up? NO! If we reduce unhealthy choices, and do what's better *most of the time,* the body will handle the rest!
- Include Healthier Habits Now
- The Palate learns simpler tastes
- Balance diet w/ light, fresh foods
- Get on the Path to More Energy
- Discover Your Lean Fit Body
- Long Term Resistance to Illness

Dietary Transition
- ✓ Opportunity to Honor Ourselves
- ✓ Cultivate new Lifelong Habits
- ✓ Be Patient with the Process
- ✓ Create Sustainable Change

Keep motivated with updates at my website www.caryellis.com for healthy lifestyle and dietary transition tips.

8

HI! I'M CARY ELLIS - WELCOME :)

My Story Starts Long Ago when chronic health challenges from helping spray an orchard as a child, gave me a huge wake-up call to recover my own health before I even turned twenty. *What could be viewed as a difficulty helped me find the gift of health!*

1970s - Inspired by *Great Pioneers*

❖ Dr. Ann Wigmore, founder original Hippocrates Health Inst. (I co-directed a branch center)

❖ Favorite health pioneer, Dr. Norman Walker, (1875-1984) began juices and raw food at fifty to recover from illness. He lived until the ripe old age of 109; author of *Natural Way to Vibrant Health* and *Become Younger.*

❖ Natural Hygiene Society, founded by Dr. Herbert Shelton promoted fasting, raw foods in the early 1900s

❖ Dr. Max Gerson's cancer therapy used successful principles (I was educator at his Mexico clinic 1978.)

I learned to cleanse inside and out, to regenerate with living foods, wheatgrass, juices. I experienced miraculous recoveries in self and others. As you might well guess, this changed my life, forever!

I was born 1952, as my uncle says, "you do the math." (2009 photo) Living a *Super Immunity Secrets* lifestyle for many years has given me long term benefits that have stood the test of time!

PURPOSE

Below in red is an important belief system about health. Put it on the refrigerator or bathroom mirror. Commit it to memory.

Being healthy is not about extremes, but finding an excellent lifestyle we can live with from day after day. Finding such Enjoyment and Consistency supports Physical, Mental, Emotional and Spiritual Well-Being.

Over many years I've run health education programs and have been on the path myself, I've watched many get enthused with an extreme approach, feel better, then slip back into their old ways. *...too bad!*

It's NOT about guilt, punishment, judgement or beating ourselves up. Changing our habits sometimes requires a friendly *boot in the rear*. See my website/blog/videos for ongoing encouragement. Spend time with others on the path, get support and essential info on dietary transition, questions answered, AND learn and integrate a healthy lifestyle *easily*.

MEANWHILE - use this book, apply what's in it, and discover a sense of greater well-being, as doors of possibility open...

> **Do nothing, you'll get nothing.**
> **Do something and -**
> **Your Life *WILL* change.**

EATING LESS ANIMAL FOODS COULD SAVE YOUR LIFE

...the diet found to reverse or eliminate all degenerative illness...
(forget high protein / low carb and other fads!)

The idea of reducing intake of meat and dairy might seem challenging, but when we're really serious about commitment to health, this information may very well help us avoid the statistics and live a longer healthier life. And change doesn't have to be extreme or sudden - it can be gradual and fun!

According to The Wall Street Journal, cancer is now passing heart disease as the world's leading killer. The question is how do we apply healthy lifestyle practices in order to increase wellness? Delicious recipes in this book offer a unique opportunity to test out proven dietary habits for yourself along with daily support at my blog, videos and classes. Amazing answers were published in the China Study (below). Plenty of information is available to help us *Get Healthy Now!*

In a 35-year study in 65 counties in China with 8,000 participants, **The China Study,** demonstrated that all degenerative illness could either be eliminated or reversed on primarily vegetarian fare, (a maximum of 7% animal foods). This isn't very much! Think: *'egg-drop soup.*

"Drawing on project findings in China, but going far beyond those findings, **The China Study** details the connection between nutrition and heart disease, diabetes and cancer. The report also examines nutritional confusion produced by powerful lobbies, government entities, and opportunistic researchers.

The New York Times has recognized the study, the *China-Oxford-Cornell Diet and Health Project,* as the "Grand Prix of epidemiology" and the "most comprehensive large study ever undertaken of the relationship between diet and the risk of developing disease."

"After a long career in research and policy-making, I've decided to step 'out of the system.' and disclose why Americans are so confused," said Dr. Colin Campbell, leader of the study and protein researcher turned vegetarian.

"As a taxpayer who foots the bill for research and health policy in America, you deserve to know that many of the common notions you have been told about food, health and disease are wrong.

"I propose to do nothing less than redefine what we think of as good nutrition. You need to know the truth about food, and why eating the right way can save your life."

TAKE CHARGE OF YOUR HEALTH NOW!

If you wrestle with challenges of change and commitment, you're not alone – our goal is to help you get grounded in an excellent lifestyle and thrive!!!

Step 1: Start with this book – **make these quick, easy** *Super Immunity Secrets* **Recipes**; learn how to include healthy ingredients everyday.

Step 2: Improve your very own path of wellness here and now. Be aware of what you eat and why. Learn and grow as you become aware. Remember, it's a process, and a journey... be patient with yourself.

THE BIG QUESTIONS

- How do we reduce animal foods?
- What do we eat?
- How do we prepare healthy food?
- How do we get enough protein?
- How to get rid of cravings?

Don't Worry! We'll make it very simple to take these steps...come along and test out the theory.

Many of my participants have overcome these common struggles:

- ➤ Social Pressure
- ➤ Family at Different Stages
- ➤ Simple Self-Discipline
- ➤ Old Habits Die Hard
- ➤ Environment
- ➤ Childhood Training
- ➤ Emotional Addictions
- ➤ Budget / Time Restraints

Remember I've walked this path too – and am here to help you get through it with tricks I've learned along the way!

Years ago, in my own dietary transition, I remember irresistibly longing for pizza – and now? I'll eat a bite in a social setting, but wouldn't make it a regular part of my diet; I've learned to love foods that are less mucous forming such as fresh fruits and salads.

Do your family and friends a favor, let them know what you're up to. It's fun to have company along the way!

ILLNESS REVERSED

I spent many years helping run alternative health education programs including the **Gerson Cancer Therapy Institute** in Mexico and a wheatgrass and living foods program in Michigan, formerly called **Hippocrates Inst.** (today **Creative Health**).

There I saw many "death sentences" reversed: a man who had a blood count low enough to be dead from leukemia regained normal count within a week on wheatgrass juice and living foods; another expelled a large tumor through his chest wall; reversal of rheumatoid arthritis with simple dietary change totally eliminating wheat and refined foods; many amazing recoveries... which helped me cultivate a belief system in the body's amazing capability to heal itself once we give it right conditions.

*Life is what happens when you're
busy making other plans.*

John Lennon

**Pay attention to what's going on around you.
Feeling good will help you take charge of your life.
Get going the direction of *YOUR DREAMS!***

INVEST IN YOUR HEALTH NOW - SAVE A FORTUNE LATER

Investing a little in your health now could save you a fortune later...

Statistics report that the *average* American spends up to $5,000+ a year on health-care. It may not be you or me at the moment, but if we don't take care of our health now it could be, later.

Join me. Have the courage, dedication and commitment to your own destiny to make your own healthy lifestyle A NUMBER ONE Priority!

In case you're wondering, we have fun learning together how to take care of ourselves and make those healthy changes! Visit us often at http://www.caryellis.com and find resources to help you on a daily basis.

Congratulations on "showing up."

I wish you well, and look forward to sharing the journey, answering your questions, and hearing about **YOUR SUCCESS!**

Life is the journey ~ not the destination

You are not alone. Learn and grow with others on the Path

FINDING SOMETHING BETTER

Making healthy changes can be easier than you think. Imagine that!

- ➢ Find Something New You Love More than the Old!
- ➢ Experiment, and Adopt a Routine You Can Live With!
- ➢ Make it Your Own Style – fun!!!
- ➢ Discover Healthy Foods *YOU Like*!
- ➢ Find and Enjoy the Company of Friends On the Same Path!
- ➢ Tell Your Story, so Others Learn too

It's fine to have a "health guru" (and there are plenty out there) telling exactly what they think we should do – but **we must make our own choices about what's good for us, listen to our body, know the right timing for our own life, grow in our own way...**

You may not live just like the "expert", but don't throw the baby out with the bath water. Take what they have to say and put it to work for you.

We grow into our own way of living healthier habits! Everyone has something to teach - take the best, leave the rest, make it work for YOU!

Chapter 2: Super Immunity Soup Recipes, Ingredients & Tips

SOUP WITHOUT MEAT?

You'd be amazed how often people ask, "Can you really make good soup without meat stock?"

Of course we can!
Maybe even better!

Making a delicious broth without meat is an art, but once you master using the *Super Immunity* Ingredients including herbs, spices and seasonings – you'll have Your Own Healthy Art Form going on.

You may find, as we do, these ingredients create such rich tasty broth that almost anything else will seem tasteless, and you will want to run home to eat your own magical soup or salad over anything!

WHAT MAKES *SUPER IMMUNITY SECRETS* RECIPES *SO* SPECIAL?

Discover Amazing Protective Properties of *Super Immunity* Ingredients on following pages. Research has shown they are like a battalion at your service to fight disease.

I wouldn't go a day without them!
I've spent many years studying ancient healing practices herbology, Ayurveda, Oriental medicine, Macrobiotics and have drawn the best from each.

Great sages understood thousands of years ago that the food we eat sustains life, creates a foundation for well-being, and plays a critical role in life, character, constitution and health.

Super Immunity concepts come from these ancient healing traditions, to serve us today as they did the wise ones of long ago.

SEND COLDS AND FLU RUNNING (*NOT YOUR NOSE*)

A delicious and powerful pot of **SUPER IMMUNITY** Soup has become the centerpiece of our home in winter, along with salads, green shakes and other yummy vegetable based meals in summer. When colds and flu are going around – we *rarely* get sick, but the best thing is we do, also know how to use herbs, homeopathy and cleansing to assist a quick recovery.

Other wellness factors besides wholesome diet include how we think and process emotions, how we live, move and have our being. Let's learn together how to consistently integrate habits that will help us avoid illness as we grow more youthful and vital by the day!

It's time to recover our understanding of how to live in harmony with the Earth and integrate this art into our modern lifestyle. This often quoted statement by Hippocrates (father of modern medicine) is as necessary today as it was 500 years ago:

~ Let your food be your medicine and your medicine be your food ~

MAGIC INGREDIENTS

Magic Ingredients are **Garlic, Ginger, Onions, Oregano, Dill, Basil, Cilantro, Rosemary, Parsley, Thyme, Curry, Cumin, Cinnamon, Coriander, and Chilies.** *These are just some of the spices and herbs that were considered priceless in ancient times, as we will discover, for good reason.*

KEEP INGREDIENTS ON HAND

These INGREDIENTS may be NEW to you, but as you get to know them, **they'll form the foundation of delightful, nourishing, protective meals on a daily basis.**

I love having Super Immunity Ingredients always available. It makes it easy to toss together a nourishing soup or salad at a moment's notice.

Use the SHOPPING LIST near the end of this book to make it easy to stock up.

SOURCES – Consider weaning yourself from those little jars at the grocery store. It's cost-wise and eco-friendly to buy in bulk, with better quality and freshness. Seek out your local natural food store or co-op for supplies. Store in your own jars. Better yet, grow your own or get fresh when available.

HERBS AND SPICES contain micro-nutrients and are more powerful blended together. Enter the art of alchemy. Read what each of these amazing foods can do for us and enjoy combining them!

As you learn about *Super Immunity Secrets*, you'll learn how to prepare protective foods for every season.

ABOUT THESE RECIPES

Anyone can make and enjoy these easy, hearty everyday meals made from easy to find nutritious ingredients. A recipe doesn't have to be exact. If you're missing one thing or another, use what you have and enjoy the creative process.

The *effort* it takes to change habits and prepare these healthy foods will pay off in the long run. Soon it will seem like you've been doing it forever!

MAKE NOW, SERVE LATER, STORAGE

LEFTOVERS With a busy schedule it's nice to make a pot of soup, heat a cup or bowl later, then freeze the rest - to thaw out for a quick meal some other day.

FREEZE Use plastic containers (recycled yogurt-type are a perfect size) for freezing left-overs soups. Label with a marker. You'll quickly learn how much you need.

One of these containers thaws on the counter during the day. When we get home at night, I heat it up, make a salad, and voilå – homemade dinner.

WORK WEEK Make a pot of soup over the weekend, freeze and use through the week. Get several batches frozen for variety.

BEANS soak, sprout, cook, put part in the freezer for next meal or pot of soup.

MEASUREMENT ABRREVIATIONS

- tsp = teaspoon
- T = tablespoon
- c = cup

EASY SPINACH GARLIC
~ SUPER IMMUNITY SECRETS ~
TIME: 30 minutes

SAUTE´ on low heat, medium soup pot:
- 3 T Olive or Coconut Oil
- 6-8 Cloves Garlic, peeled, sliced

When it turns golden and smells delicious, add 6 cups water to pot, bring to simmer.

Add Super Immunity Ingredients

- ½ tsp Cumin
- ½ tsp Curry Powder
- 2 tsp. Oregano
- 1 tsp Basil
- ½ tsp Chili Powder
- 3 Green Onions or Scallions sliced
- 1 stalk Celery thinly sliced

Turn off heat - add

- Spinach 1 bunch washed, chopped
- 1 bunch chopped Cilantro
- Juice of a lime or lemon
- 1-2 T Soy Sauce
- 1 tsp Umeboshi Plum Vinegar
- Sprinkle thinly sliced green onions

Stir – spinach and herbs will be wilted.

SERVE with healthy crackers.

Sprinkle with grated soy or rice cheese

GARLIC - enjoy white, purple, large, small and garlic chives or spring greens.

Cultivated for 5,000 years, garlic was used by the Egyptians for strength and endurance. Studies show:

- *Allicin* – potent antibiotic similar to penicillin
- Potent remedy for common cold, University of Munich found garlic reduced replication of viruses including HIV, by stopping NF-Kappa B, response to inflammatory illness
- Antibodies higher w/eat raw & cooked garlic regularly, lower in those who avoid it
- Lowers risk of several common cancers
- Supports healthy blood pressure, serum triglycerides, platelet aggregation, cholesterol
- Prevents atherosclerosis, diabetic heart disease
- Reduces risk of heart attack and stroke
- Lessens free radicals, plaque, triglycerides
- Relaxes blood vessels, lowers blood pressure
- Contains selenium, which provides protection against cancer and heavy metal toxicity
- Potent against resistant strains such as *staph*
- Contains organic *sulphur* compounds amazingly effective against skin cancer
- Phytonutrient responsible for pungency blocks cancer causing compounds, particularly those from high meat consumption resulting in breast cancer
- *Allium* vegetables - garlic onion families contain two potent protective antioxidant enzymes, glutathione and SOD which reduce risk of prostate, breast, colon cancers
- Is DNA protective with asbestos exposure
- Assists w/weight control, lowers insulin

Research references on page 66

GINGER - most markets these days carry fresh ginger root. Look for it and love it – a great healing food. Native to southeast Asia, Rome imported ginger from China 2,000 years ago. Ginger is widely used in many cultures - Mediterranean, West Indies, Mexico and South America.

Put chunks into soup, remove when done as it can be spicy - or enjoy its pungent taste! Extensive studies show ginger to have these health benefits:

- Stimulates digestion
- Relieves gas and soothes intestinal tract
- Is antioxidant for free radical protection
- Conserves *glutathion,* essential cell protectant
- *Gingerol compounds* anti-inflammatory
- Osteoarthritis - double-blind study - reduces pain and swelling, increases mobility
- Relieves motion and sea-sickness including dizziness, nausea, cold sweats (tested superior to *Dramamine*)
- Reduces even extreme nausea of pregnancy with a small dose and no side effects
- Extracts protect against tumors
- Causes death of ovarian cancer cells
- Inhibits growth of colorectal cancer
- Immune boosting

Eating ginger daily opens receptivity.

Confucius

Simmer a few slices of ginger in water for delightful spicy tea.

EASY ORIENTAL NOODLE
~ SUPER IMMUNITY SECRETS ~
TIME: 30 minutes

Heat large soup pot with 2 quarts water

Add Super Immunity Ingredients
- 3 Green Onions, sliced thin
- 3 Cloves Garlic, peeled, sliced or crushed
- 1" fresh Ginger, sliced thin, chopped fine
- ½ tsp Crushed Red Pepper
- 1 tsp Dill Weed
- 1 tsp Oregano

Add:
- Sugar Snap Peas
- Red Pepper – cut into long slivers
- Finely Shredded Green Cabbage
- Thin Rice or Bean Thread Noodles, broken

2-3 T Toasted Sesame Oil or Olive Oil
- 2 T Soy Sauce
- 1 tsp Umeboshi Plum Vinegar

Turn off heat. Let sit for 5 minutes.

Top each bowl with: Diced ripe avocado and sprouts,. Serve with fresh salad

NOTE: You'll love these noodles. Find in oriental section at supermarket. Good for those with food sensitivities; lean cookin'.

This is original "fast food" – these noodles generally take almost no cooking – when dropped into the simmering pot, turn off heat, let sit a few minutes and they are ready to eat; a great choice for the busy person "on the go".

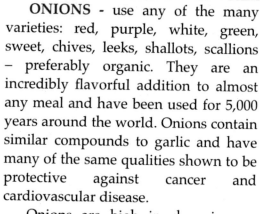

EVERYDAY VEGETABLE NOODLE
(Kids' Favorite)
~ SUPER IMMUNITY SECRETS ~
TIME: 30 minutes

HEAT large soup pot with 2.5 qts water

Bring to boil and stir while adding:

- 1# of your favorite pasta-such as bow ties, *rigatoni, penne regate* (experiment w/whole grain varieties)
- 3 Scallions or Green Onions – sliced
- 1 Large Carrot – quartered, sliced thin
- 1 Bunch Parsley washed, chopped (save some for garnish)
- 2 Cloves Garlic – peeled, diced

Add Super Immunity Ingredients

- 1 tsp Dill Weed
- 1 tsp Oregano
- ½ tsp Thyme
- ½ tsp Curry Powder
- ¼ tsp Coriander
- ¼ tsp Earth or Sea Salt

Simmer 10-20 minutes or till pasta and vegetables are tender.

As cooking add:
- 2 T Soy Sauce
- 3 T Toasted Sesame Oil

- Garnish with fresh chopped Parsley or Cilantro

SERVE immediately. For a traditional style meal, serve with soy cheese grilled sandwiches on hearty multi-grain bread or tortillas.

ONIONS - use any of the many varieties: red, purple, white, green, sweet, chives, leeks, shallots, scallions – preferably organic. They are an incredibly flavorful addition to almost any meal and have been used for 5,000 years around the world. Onions contain similar compounds to garlic and have many of the same qualities shown to be protective against cancer and cardiovascular disease.

Onions are high in chromium, a mineral essential insulin response; clinical tests show onions lower blood sugar levels by increasing the amount of available free insulin by occupying sites in the liver where insulin is inactivated.

Research demonstrates benefits of the mighty onion:

- ❖ Similar sulphur containing compounds to garlic, basis of antibiotic factors
- ❖ Reduces glucose in glucose tolerance tests
- ❖ Lowers high cholesterol and blood pressure
- ❖ Loweres risk for heart attack and stroke
- ❖ Reduces risk colon cancer via flavonoid quercitin also found in turmeric
- ❖ Reduces risk of many common cancers
- ❖ Reduces risk of ovarian cancer
- ❖ Helps maintain healthy bones
- ❖ Reduces arthritic inflammation and swelling
- ❖ Anti-inflammatory
- ❖ Kills harmful bacteria associated w/ colds, flu

QUICK CREAMY BROCCOLI
~ SUPER IMMUNITY SECRETS ~
TIME: 30 minutes

In medium soup pot steam with lid until broccoli is bright green:

- 1 large onion diced
- 2 cups chopped broccoli
- 2-4 cloves garlic crushed or diced

Blend in blender then add to pot:

- 2 cups water
- 3 T Flour (whole grain best)
- 2 T Olive Oil

Add, stir, simmer till slightly thick:
- 3 cups Almond or Soy Milk
- ½ tsp Cumin
- ½ tsp Curry Powder
- 2 tsp Dill Weed
- 1 tsp Oregano
- ½ tsp Red Chili powder
- ¼ tsp Coriander

Add last minute of cooking (mix first)
- 1 T Miso and ¼ c Water
Or substitute 2 T Soy Sauce

OPT - blend all or part in blender, hold lid with towel, start on low. Caution hot!

Serve into bowls. Top with
Pinch Dill Weed, Red Chili Pepper, Small Broccoli Floretd

ENJOY with a salad and healthy crackers.
Try a dollop of plain non-dairy or organic yogurt on top.

OREGANO - an amazing herb, once you start using it you'll never want to be without it again. Its rich aromatic intoxicating scent and flavor (familiar from pizza) will make your everyday foods irresistible.

Perennial plant (comes back every year), cultivate in your yard; find dried oregano that is fresh and pungent. Studies have shown oregano to have protective qualities:

- ❖ Inhibits growth of bacteria & *staph*
- ❖ Mexican studies found oregano more effective against *giardia* than drugs commonly used
- ❖ Potent antioxidant
- ❖ Nutrient rich
- ❖ Oil found to be effective against *herpes*

Historically cultivated in France in the Middle Ages; oregano crowned brides and grooms as a perennial symbol of joy in ancient Greece and Rome.
Use heaping spoonfuls of these herbs dried in soups, and fresh snipped leaves in salads!

DILL WEED hails from ancient Greece; same family as cumin, parsley and bay, adds delightful fresh flavor. Research reports the following qualities:

- ❖ Activates glutathione, anti-oxidant
- ❖ Chemoprotective - neutralizes carcinogens
- ❖ Anti-bacterial
- ❖ Source of calcium, reduces bone loss

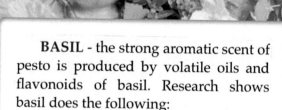

SUPER VEGETARIAN VEGGIE
~ SUPER IMMUNITY SECRETS ~
TIME: 30 minutes

SAUTE´ in soup pot:
- 2 T Olive Oil
- 1 Onion, diced
- 3-4 cloves Garlic, peeled, whole
- ½-1 cup sliced Mushrooms

When smells delicious add 2 qts water and Add what you have on hand below:
- 1-2" chunk Ginger Root (remove later – opt);
- 1-2 lg Carrots, diced; cubed Yam/Sweet Potato;
- 2-3 Red Potatoes cubed; 1 Parsnip, chopped;
- Broccoli chopped small; fresh or frozen Peas;
- Green Beans; Corn – cut off cob
- Washed chopped Parsley

Add Super Immunity Secrets™ Ingredients
- ½ tsp Cumin
- 1 tsp Curry Powder
- 1 T Oregano
- 1 tsp Basil
- ½ tsp Thyme
- Large handful washed chopped Parsley
- ½ tsp crushed Red Chili

Simmer till potatoes are tender, then add:
- 2-3 T Coconut Oil (or Olive Oil)
- 1 T Miso (mixed w/¼ c water) or 2 T Soy Sauce
- 1 tsp Umeboshi Plum Vinegar
- Handful chopped Cilantro

SERVE w/multi-grain crackers, top w/crumbled tofu or non-dairy or organic yogurt.

BASIL - the strong aromatic scent of pesto is produced by volatile oils and flavonoids of basil. Research shows basil does the following:
- Supports structure of white blood cells
- Protects chromosomes from radiation damage
- Antibacterial against *staph* and resistant bacteria
- Anti-inflammatory similar to many over-the-counter anti-inflammatory drugs
- Rids fresh produce of food borne bacteria
- High in vitamin K.

CILANTRO – leaf of the Coriander plant (refer to qualities listed for coriander).

A Japanese dentist, performing urine tests on patients before and after silver-mercury filling removal, discovered that when eating soup for lunch with cilantro, patients eliminated large amounts of mercury.

Much electricity in the modern world comes from coal burning power plants, which produce 40% of the mercury pollution in our atmosphere. Most of us have chronic mercury exposure either from the atmosphere or from old silver fillings, which makes this herb essential to our regular diet.

Put cilantro on your grocery list. Add to soups and salads. Grow it. Re-seeds easily in garden or flowerpot.

ROSEMARY stimulates the immune system, increases circulation, improves digestion; anti-inflammatory, stimulates circulation to the brain, improves memory; shown beneficial in asthma.

Ancient Greeks wore rosemary in their hair, it was tossed as remembrance for the dead, and symbolized fidelity.

Rosemary grows as an evergreen shrub, related to mint, perennial in many climates. Much better fresh than dried, keep a plant and snip the fresh needle-like leaves. I love having a pot in a sunny spot in the house for winter use.

PARSLEY inhibits tumor formation (animal studies with lung tumors), is "chemo-protective" – can neutralize certain carcinogens; increases antioxidants, and is extremely high in vitamins A, K & C. Every trip to the grocery store from our house brings back parsley.

THYME conserves DHA (omega 3 fatty-acid) levels in cells of brain, kidney and heart; anti-aging, antioxidant flavonoids, antibacterial against *staph* and *shigella*; helps decontaminate foods of microbial contamination.

IN A HURRY SPICED UP RAMEN
Wayward Men and College Students
~ SUPER IMMUNITY SECRETS ~
TIME: 10 minutes – and out the door

You know those packages of *Ramen* noodles sold at the market and health food store for pretty cheap (many brands). Find the ones with NO MSG – read the ingredients on label. Keep these around with frozen veggies, herbs and spices for homemade "fast food."

Heat soup pot with 1 quart water and
1-2 packages Ramen Noodles broken up

Toss in whatever you have:
- 1 Green Onion, sliced thin
- 1-2 cloves Garlic – crushed or diced
- 1-2 thin slices Ginger Root
- ½ tsp Dill Weed, Oregano or Basil
- Washed chopped Cilantro or Parsley
- ½ tsp Curry Powder
- ½ tsp Crushed Red Chilies or Powder

Frozen Veggies of choice:
French Cut Green Beans, Peas or...

Raw:
- Chopped Broccoli
- Finely Shredded Green or Purple Cabbage
- Diced Red or Yellow Sweet Pepper

Add:
- 1-2 T Soy Sauce
- 2 T Toasted Sesame Oil or Olive Oil

Top with diced Ripe Avocado...mmmm
**You get the idea. Get a spoon.
Breathe...Enjoy. Have a great day!**

CURRY - famous flavor of the far east, consists of various blends containing turmeric, chilies, cumin and other spices. Its primary ingredient, turmeric, has been considered powerful medicine by both Chinese and Indian systems of healing for centuries; used to treat a wide variety of conditions, such as jaundice, menstrual difficulties, flatulence, bloody urine, hemorrhage, toothache, bruises, chest pain, colic. Modern studies demonstrate the following:

- Both the volatile oil and pigment of turmeric have been shown to have **anti-inflammatory qualities equal to the drug hydrocortisone.**
- Studies show *curicumin*, the yellow-orange pigment, may offer the possibility of inexpensive, effective, well-tolerated treatment for:
  ✓ ulcerative colitis; inflammatory bowel diseases
  ✓ Crohns disease
  ✓ rheumatoid arthritis
  ✓ prostate cancer
  ✓ childhood leukemia
  ✓ cystic fibrosis
  ✓ destructive to mutating cancer cells
  ✓ inhibits cancer growth and metastases

How about on scrambled eggs, sprinkled on salads, and definitely a good amount in yummy SUPER IMMUNITY SOUPS!

SPROUTED LENTIL MAGIC
~ SUPER IMMUNITY SECRETS ~
TIME: 30 min. (plus sprouting)

I CALL THEM MAGIC because sprouted lentils are an inexpensive live food – that anyone can do!

TO SPROUT YOUR LENTILS GET:
a. Wide Mouth (1-2 quart canning jars from hardware, thrift store or Grandma's
b. Big Rubber Band or Ring Lid
c. Piece screen, cheesecloth, or stocking

HOW TO SPROUT -
- Soak 2 c Lentils in jar, water to cover
- Put screen on top, rubber band or ring lid
- Drain after 6-10 hrs. (upsidedown)
- Rinse, drain a.m. & p.m. daily – 2-3 days
- May keep in refrigerator up to a week

MAKE SOUP - Simmer 2 qts water and
- 1 Onion, peeled, diced
- 4 cloves Garlic, peeled, diced
- 1-2 large Carrots, diced small
- 2- 1" chunks Ginger (remove later)
- ½ tsp Cumin
- 1 tsp Curry Powder
- 1 T Oregano
- 1 tsp Basil
- ½ tsp Thyme
- Rosemary
- Large handful washed chopped Parsley
- ½ tsp red Chili Powder
- ½ tsp green Chili Powder
- 4-6 cups Sprouted Lentils

ADD when almost done:
Chopped Spinach and Cilantro, 2-3 T olive oil, 1 T miso (mixed into ¼ c water)

Take lentils on long river trips such as Grand Canyon and grow your own fresh food, AMAZING AND FUN!!!

MOUTH-WATERING MUSHROOM
~ SUPER IMMUNITY SECRETS ~
TIME: 30 minutes

SAUTE: in medium soup pot:
- 3 T Coconut Oil or Toasted Sesame Oil
- 6 cloves Garlic, peeled, crushed or diced
- 1# Cremini or Button Mushrooms, sliced

Add 1 quart water and simmer

Add Super Immunity Secrets™ Ingredients
- 1 T Oregano
- 1 tsp Dill Weed
- ¼ tsp Thyme
- ½ tsp Cumin
- pinch Cinnamon
- ½ tsp Green Chili Powder

In skillet, melt & stir in till just golden:
- 3T Coconut Oil or Organic Butter
- 3 T Flour (whole wheat, oat, spelt, white)
- ¼ tsp Sea or Earth Salt

Whisk in thoroughly till no lumps (blend in blender if needed)
- 2 cups plain Almond, Hazelnut or Soy Milk

Add to above soup. Stir and simmer 5 minutes or so till thickened.

SERVE w/Sprout Salad and crusty Bread spread with Coconut Oil or Organic Butter.

CUMIN - often a component of Curry and excellent alone is a vital ingredient in Mexico, the Middle East and India. Cumin is high in iron, stimulates digestion, and scavenges free radicals to support liver function. It adds a hearty taste to foods, especially good in beans. Common use of Cumin may contribute largely to Mexico's low cancer rate.

CINNAMON contains essential oils effective in anti-clotting. It stops the growth of bacteria, fungi and *candida*; helps lessen impact of high carb foods on blood sugar levels, and assists adults with type 2 diabetes improve insulin response – and it tastes good, too!

CORIANDER This sweet, tasty seed of cilantro, is known in Europe as the anti-diabetic plant. It's been used in India for anti-inflammatory properties, and in the U.S. has been studied for cholesterol-lowering qualities. All three properties have been proven in recent experiments; also contains powerful phytonutrients and flavonoids. U.S. and Mexican researchers found it to be twice as effective as drugs at killing salmonella; also contains 8 other antibiotic compounds. It has a sweet flavor; I like to use along with or in place of Cinnamon with apples, but is also an excellent addition to savory soups, salad and grain dishes.

CHILIES – there are many varieties of Chili, all containing a potent substance called *capsaicin*, a potent inhibitor of the neuropeptide associated with inflammatory process, extremely effective in pain relief, with cardiovascular benefits, clearing congestion, boosting immunity used with high doses of vitamins A and C; proven to stop the growth of prostate cancer. Regular use reduces insulin requirements, kills stomach bacteria that may lead to ulcers, increases thermogenesis, assists with weight loss.

BLENDS of chili powders contain additional ingredients such as oregano, cumin and garlic powder. In these recipes I am **just calling for plain ground chili powder red or green**; if you use a blend, make your adjustment. I generally keep mild to medium around and just add more for spicy flavor (be cautious with hot chilies). Find chilies at your supermarket in the Mexican food section.

Many chilies can be purchased fresh in season. I get roasted green chilies in the fall and freeze for winter, though dried plain chili is a great mainstay. If you have a hard time finding dried green chili – substitute frozen. Crushed red chilies generally have the seeds in them – and are not as fine as the powdered (wonderful addition to soups in moderation).

How about chili and chocolate? Sounds crazy? It's seriously good!

GREEN CHILI STEW
~ SUPER IMMUNITY SECRETS ~
TIME: 30 minutes

SAUTE´ in medium soup pot:
- 3 T Olive Oil
- 1 large Onion diced
- 3-4 cloves Garlic, peeled, crushed or diced

Add:
- 1 quart Water
- 1 large Carrot quartered and diced small
- 1 Potato diced small (opt)
- ½ - ¾ cup chopped, roasted Green Chilies (fresh or frozen)
- 1/2 tsp Curry powder
- ½ tsp Cumin
- ½ tsp Coriander
- ½ tsp Thyme
- 1 tsp Oregano
- ½ tsp Dill Weed

Simmer till potatoes are tender.

Brown lightly in skillet:
- 4 T Coconut Oil (Organic Butter. Olive Oil)
- 1/2 cup Oat Flour can blend rolled oats in blender to make flour

Whisk or stir into flour mixture:
- 1 cup broth (above)
- 2 T Soy Sauce
- Pinch Sea or Earth Salt

Scrape flour/broth mixture into blender, blend till smooth, caution hot. Add to soup pot, stir and simmer till thickened.

Garnish:
Chopped Cilantro, wedge of Lime. Optional: Grated Rice or Soy Cheddar Cheese

Chili - essential ingredient of the southwest.

"Fat free" may not be all it's cracked up to be.

HEALTHY FAT AND OIL – We require regular intake of healthy fats to create energy, nourish cells and burn the "bad" fat. This becomes particularly noticeable when we lower our intake of animal foods. Often we think we need protein when what we really need is healthy fat. Olive oil and avocado contain mono-saturated oils thought to lower bad LDL cholesterol and raise the good HDL. These are some of the finest fats found in nature, along with raw nuts and seeds, and should be part of our daily regimen, particularly raw.

Coconut oil was given a bad rap in the 1950s when manufacturers of polyunsaturated vegetable oils wanted a corner on the market and discouraged consumers from buying coconut oil. What we really need to avoid like the plague is processed shortening and margarines, which contain trans-fat, heavy metals and other impurities that contribute to Alzheimers and cardiovascular disease.

Coconut oil contains monolauren, a beneficial fatty acid with antiviral antibacterial qualities, effective against microorganisms such as candida. It contains medium chain fatty acids and is absorbed and burned for energy, rather than getting stored in fat cells. Monolauren is thought to improve cognitive function in type 1 diabetes and hypoglycemia, as well as improve cardiovascular health.

Coconut oil has also been found to have a positive effect on the thyroid, raising metabolism for leanness and weight loss. Be sure to buy the most natural, cold processed coconut oil and olive oil you can afford.

You will find these beneficial fats make soups much more tasty, nourishing and sustaining. Add them near the end of cooking time so they are basically raw. Also add some during cooking as the oil assists to draw compounds from the herbs and spices to make them more available.

Toasted sesame oil adds a wonderful flavor and is part of the macrobiotic tradition. Shown to be beneficial for heart and kidneys it contains antioxidants, is protective of DNA, raises interleukin levels (disease fighting component of the blood), and is cancer protective particularly agains skin cancer and leukemia.

ABOUT DAIRY - If you consume dairy, please BUY ORGANIC. If you haven't yet seen it, watch the Michael Moore movie, *The Corporation*. It offers essential information regarding disease in commercial dairy production and manipulation of information by food producer's associations. Again, vote with your grocery bill when you can for organic food; it may cost a little more now but less in the long run.

SALT

A little salt goes a long way – reduce salt intake, and use "whole" mineralized salt when you do. We don't call for it often in a recipe, though grains and beans may be enhanced with a tiny bit of salt.

Make a trip to your local health food store and explore the wonderful world of highly mineralized sea and earth salts – solar dried. There's a reason ancient cultures traveled and traded for salt.

Today, more than ever with the demineralization of soils, natural earth or sea salt with a spectrum of minerals and trace minerals, is found beneficial in small quantities.

Dr. Bernard Jensen in *Health Magic Through Chlorophyll*, tells the story of pygmies in Africa trading anything for salt, but once they had fresh greens added to their diet, salt lost its value. Taste buds often come alive when meat intake is reduced and replaced with living vital foods.

More fresh and raw fruits and vegetables in the diet, particularly organic, will nourish the body with minerals in their most vital and available form. When using unsprouted grains and beans, a little salt enhances taste, but you'll be amazed at the tiny amount of salt you really need with vital foods.

DREAMY POTATO

~ SUPER IMMUNITY SECRETS ~

TIME: 15 min prep, cook 1+ hour

BROTH:

Heat large soup pot with 2 quarts water

Add and simmer -

- 4-6 Potatoes cut in bite-sized cubes
- 1-2 Sweet Potatoes or Yams cubed
- 2 large Carrots, cubed (opt)
- 1 large Onion, peeled, diced
- 3-4 Cloves Garlic – diced, sliced or crushed
- Handful washed, chopped Parsley
- 1" chunk Ginger Root (remove later)
- ½ tsp crushed Red Pepper
- 1 tsp Dill Weed
- 1+ tsp Curry Powder
- ¼-1/2 tsp Earth or Sea Salt
- ½ tsp Cumin
- ½ tsp Coriander

When potatoes are tender, add

- 1-2 cups Plain Almond, Hazelnut or Soy Milk
- 2 tsp Miso mix w/water (or 2 T Soy Sauce)
- 3 T Olive Oil and/or 3 T Coconut Oil

BLEND small portions at a time, return to pot, and then blend more until you have the smoothness or chunkiness you desire. Caution hot - hold blender top w/towel, blend on low speed.

Top with a pinch of Dill Weed, Red Chili Powder, Thin curl of carrot or Parsley

SERVE - with fresh cabbage salad.

GARNISH with grated Rice Cheese or Soy Cheese or Organic Cheddar

INSTANT MISO
~ SUPER IMMUNITY SECRETS ~
TIME: 10 minutes

Favorite Japanese "fast food", Miso soup is a standby, protective, healing food; quick, easy to prepare, healthy, light, nourishing and delicious.

Bring 2 c water to boil per person - ADD ANY OF THE FOLLOWING:

- Sliced Green Onions
- Crushed Garlic Cloves
- Grated Carrot (or very thinly sliced)
- Chopped Cilantro
- Washed, chopped Parsley
- Washed, chopped Raw Spinach
- Frozen Peas (or other frozen veggies)

Simmer 5 min – till veggies barely tender

Add during the last 2 minutes:

- Rinsed Tofu, crumbled or diced

Turn off heat and add (per 2 cups water):

- 1 tsp White or Red Miso (dissolved in 1/4 c water first)
- 1 tsp Umeboshi Plum Vinegar
- 1T Toasted Sesame Oil or Olive Oil

Top with any of these:

- Sliced Green Onions
- Chopped Cilantro
- Alfalfa or Mung Bean Sprouts

Enjoy with Rollups *(see Light Fare)*

NUTRITIOUS FLAVORS FROM THE ORIENT

Umeboshi Plums and Plum Vinegar have a very salty sour taste (a little goes a long way). Great chefs say good food has salty, sweet, sour, bitter and pungent flavors – and sour is often missing. Alternative to Umeboshi Plum Vinegar, either paste or whole plums can be used.

Ume Plum, from Japan, is called "king of alkalizing foods," used in ancient times to balance and strengthen. Esteemed by Samurai to combat battle fatigue. Served in Japan with rice to fight colds and flu. China and Asia also have similar varieties, dried in the sun.

Soy Sauce is fermented and adds a savory flavor (nice replacement for meat broth). Find a natural brand of soy sauce, add to enhance flavor.

Nama Shoyu, is raw soy sauce, not easy to find, but a favorite when I can get it; always add last so the living enzymes survive.

Miso is a paste made from fermented soybeans and grains. It adds wonderful flavor to soups. Add during last minute of cooking to preserve live enzymes.

Experiment with light and dark miso – find flavors you like and keep refrigerated. A little goes a long way so use sparingly in soup broth and for seasoning.

Hiroshima survivors who ate miso soup daily were less sick – demonstrating protective factors.

Find at health food or oriental store.

PREPARED WITH LOVE

Have you ever noticed how "lacking life" food tastes from many restaurants compared with something made by mom, a friend, our beloved or ourselves?

This is very real stuff. Realize above all else that energy is more powerful than matter. In fact, quantum physics teaches us that matter moves into form as a result of intention placed upon it.

I know this is all rather heady to think about – but in simple terms – what we think and feel as food is prepared and taken into the body directly affects our health and well-being. The radiance of love, healing and caring is carried by food and water – and transmitted to us – to help us be more alive.

Contemplate this for a moment...

TRY THIS. *Turn off the TV ... put on peaceful music you enjoy ... breathe ... smile... enter into pleasant conversation ... as you prepare or eat food with awareness, imagine your cells (and those with you) receiving it in good health ... notice what happens...*

BODY WISDOM

You've probably heard it before - now it's time to do it:
- ✓ Listen to *your* body
- ✓ Discover healthy "cravings"
- ✓ Eat what you love
- ✓ Eat small amounts
- ✓ Step away when full
- ✓ Climb the Transitional Ladder
  (get Cary's chart while they last)
- ✓ Bring Awareness into all that you do
- ✓ Become fully present in the now...

EAT WITH THE SEASONS / CLIMATE

These are *WARMING* soups to enjoy during cooler weather. As our food needs change with the seasons. Warm nourishing *SUPER IMMUNITY SOUPS* will cozy up your winter, spring or fall.

Eat according to climate and season, with lighter more raw foods for warmer climates and warmer days as you enjoy exciting salads and light fare recipes later in this book.

Ancient traditions and Earth wisdom teach us to eat locally grown, organic in season. Obviously it's not so simple, as anything can be shipped to our door. In general if we live in a cold-winter climate we may require more calorically dense foods such as grains, beans potatoes, winter squash and other root crops during the colder months.

If we live in a warm climate these foods may be too heavy, and we will be satisfied with fresh and raw fruits, veggies, nuts and other magical things picked in their natural state.

EASY AROMATIC ONION
~ SUPER IMMUNITY SECRETS~
TIME: 30 minutes

CROUTONS:
Spread Coconut Oil or Olive Oil or Organic Butter on hearty Whole Grain Bread slices.

Cut into cubes on cookie sheet – bake at 250° till crunchy (15-20 min).

SAUTE´ in medium soup pot
- 3 T Coconut Oil or Olive Oil or Toasted Sesame Oil
- 2 Large Sweet Onions – peeled and sliced into rings
- 2 T Oregano
- 4 Cloves Garlic peeled and sliced

Once softened and somewhat translucent Add 6-8 cups water to pot and bring to simmer

Add Super Immunity Ingredients
- ½ tsp Cumin
- Several springs Rosemary
- ½ tsp Red or Green Chili Powder
- 1 bunch Parsley washed, chopped fine
- ½ tsp Curry Powder

Simmer 10 minutes or so till flavors are melded, smells wonderful.

SERVE with Croutons, sliced green onions. grated Rice, Soy or Organic Cheese or whatever you like.

CHOOSING PRODUCE

Whenever possible choose what seems the most fresh and vibrant available – use eyes and hands to look for bright colors, feel for ripeness. As your taste becomes more refined, it will tell you how good your produce really is. Vote for the future with your choices.

➢ BUY LOCAL
  • Farmers' market
  • Natural foods store
  • Grow your own garden –

➢ BUY ORGANIC
  • Farmers or natural foods market
  • Often available at supermarket today

➢ EAT HIGH LIFE FORCE
  • Sprouted
  • Fresh
  • Dehydrated
  • Frozen
  • Canned

Notice the feeling as you read this list...

TASTE TEST

Food that's been grown organically and on good soil will taste AMAZINGLY better - with more highly developed sugars, proteins and greater mineral content. Once you start eating this way you will become learn to love natural organic foods.

With each recipe taste test before you serve. You'll learn over time how to make adjustments to get the taste just right for your household.

QUICK TOMATO
~ SUPER IMMUNITY SECRETS ~
TIME: 15 minutes

In summer we make raw tomato soup. If you have raw tomatoes in the winter, by all means please use them instead of canned. For the average budget, canned tomatoes may be more readily available during winter months.

Heat on low in medium soup pot:
• 3 T Coconut Oil (or Olive Oil)

Add and sauté lightly till golden:
• 1 medium Purple Onion, diced
• 3-4 cloves Garlic, peeled and sliced

Add to pot and simmer:
• 3 cups Water
• 1 large can Diced Tomatoes (28 oz)

Add Super Immunity Seasonings
• 1 T Oregano
• ½ tsp crushed Red Chilies
• 2 tsp Basil (if you have fresh, load it up)
• ½ tsp Cumin
• ½ tsp Coriander
• Sprinkle Cinnamon

SERVE top with crumbled tofu, or dollop of plain organic yogurt. Have a slice of crunchy sprouted whole grain toast with coconut oil spread on it. Yum!

SO EASY MINESTRONE
~ SUPER IMMUNITY SECRETS ~
TIME: 30 minutes

Heat in medium soup pot and simmer till pasta is tender (10-20 min):

4 quarts water
- 1 can (28 oz) Diced Tomatoes
- 1 can (15 oz) Great Northern Beans (or some you cooked)
- 1 Onion, diced
- 1 Carrot – quartered, sliced very thin
- 4 Cloves Garlic, peeled and diced
- 1 cup Small Pasta Shells or Macaroni (try whole grain) or other small pasta on hand
- 1 T Oregano
- ½ tsp Thyme
- Few sprigs Rosemary
- ½ tsp crushed Red Pepper
- ½ tsp Coriander
- ½ tsp Cumin
- Pinch Salt
- Broccoli florets
- 1 bunch Parsley washed, chopped

Add last:
- 3 T Olive Oil
- 2-3 T Soy Sauce

SERVE with sliced tomatoes on leaf lettuce with Olive Oil and Umeboshi Plum Vinegar, sprinkled with Oregano; cubes of rice, soy or organic mozzarella cheese.

QUICK SPINACH NOODLE
~ SUPER IMMUNITY SECRETS ~
TIME: 30 minutes

Bring 1 1/2 quarts water to boil in soup pot.

Cut and add:
- 1 small Onion – diced
- 2-3 Garlic Cloves, peeled or crushed
- 1" chunk Ginger Root (remove later)
- Sliced Carrots
- 1/2 c cooked or canned Garbanzo Beans

Super Immunity Ingredients
- 1 tsp Curry Powder
- 1 tsp Dill Weed
- 1 tsp Rosemary (few sprigs)
- ½ tsp Thyme
- ¼ tsp Sea Salt
- ½ tsp Red or Green Chili Powder
- Pinch Earth or Sea Salt

Break into 1"-2" pieces as you drop into boiling water and stir:
- ½ # Angel Hair Pasta

Add while simmering:
- Several handfuls chopped Spinach
- 2-3 T Toasted Sesame, Coconut, Olive Oil
- 2 T Soy Sauce

Turn off heat.
Ladle into bowls.
Top with:
- Chopped fresh Cilantro
- Chopped fresh Red Pepper

SERVE Mmmm… enjoy with other healthy favorites – such as nori or lettuce wraps.

THAI NOODLE
~ SUPER IMMUNITY SECRETS ~
TIME: 30 minutes

BROTH
Start in large soup pot with 2-3 quarts water.

Add

Super Immunity Secrets™ Ingredients
- 1 large Onion, peeled, diced
- 4 cloves Garlic, peeled, diced
- 2-3 large chunks Ginger root (remove after cooking)
- 2 heaping Tablespoons Oregano
- 1 heaping teaspoon Curry powder
- 1 teaspoon Cumin
- ½ teaspoon Green and/or Red Chili powder
- 1 teaspoon crushed Red Chili
- 1 teaspoon Dill Weed

Simmer ½ hour or so till ingredients are melded.

Turn off heat.

Add about
- 4 cups fine Rice Noodles

(find in the oriental section of your market/ or natural food store).
Break them up with your hands to make easier to eat. If you use fine noodles they just need to soak in the hot broth (not cook).

If you are using a heavier noodle you may need to simmer a few minutes with the noodles. If you don't have rice noodles, feel free to replace with any pasta and simmer for the length of time suggested.

Add and stir in:
- 1 bunch fresh Spinach, wash, chop a little
- ½ Bell Pepper diced (red, orange or yellow)
- ½ bunch chopped fresh Cilantro
-
- 1-2 T natural, organic Soy Sauce
- 2 T Toasted Sesame Oil or Cold Pressed, Virgin Olive Oil
- 1 t Umeboshi Plum Vinegar

Sprinkle with a little thinly sliced Green Onion

TASTE AND SERVE with lime wedges and a fresh cucumber/seaweed salad, or fresh salad of your choice.

WINElabel...

WINTER SQUASH or PUMPKIN
~ SUPER IMMUNITY SECRETS ~
TIME: prep ½ hour, cooking 1 hour

BROTH: Start in large soup pot with 2 quarts water.

Add 3-4 cups squash or pumpkin (above)

Add *Super Immunity Secrets™ Ingredients*
- 1 Onion, peeled, diced
- 2 cloves Garlic, peeled, diced
- 2 chunks Ginger root (remove after cooking)
- 1 heaping T Oregano
- 1 tsp Curry Powder
- ½ tsp Cumin
- 1 tsp Coriander
- ½ tsp Cinnamon
- ½ tsp Green or Red Chili powder
- 1 tsp crushed Red Chili
- 1 tsp Dill Weed

Simmer at least ½ hour or so till ingredients are melded.
Turn off heat. Remove ginger chunks if you wish.

When cooled a little, blend the soup in blender with (*hold lid on blender with towel - hot!*)
- 2 cups Plain Almond, Hazelnut or Soy Milk

Return to pot and add remaining 3 cups or so of baked/chunked squash or pumpkin. Warm up again. Add and stir in:
- 1 T natural, organic Soy Sauce
- 1 T cold pressed, virgin Olive Oil

Serve into bowls and top with
- Chopped fresh Cilantro
- Finely sliced Green Onion
- A pinch of ground Coriander

TASTE AND SERVE with crusty whole grain bread and fresh salad of choice.

Preparing Winter Squash

Use any winter squash or pumpkin available in season, preferably organic, to make this great fall or winter soup.

When you shop at your local farm, farmers market or natural foods grocery you'll discover all kinds of winter squashes you've never seen before – try some, they are super good!

Start out by placing the squash(s) you have on a large baking sheet and bake at 300° till tender (about 1 hr.). If large pumpkin or squash cut it in half to bake more quickly.

When tender, remove from oven, let cool a little. Scoop out seeds, put on baking sheet and season with a little olive oil, sea salt, soy sauce and bake at 250° till crunchy. Alternate raw version: remove seeds, dehydrate with seasonings.

Then cut up or spoon out the the squash and add to broth below. Use about ½ the squash to simmer with the broth and add the rest later after blending the soup for a chunky texture.

GREAT GRAIN VARIETIES

Many grains (seeds of grasses) from around the world have provided basic sustenance for thousands of years. Get organic at your natural food store.

Each has slightly different preparation requirements. In other places I teach more about sprouted grains – but for our purposes here we will use grains in their dry form to add to soups, which is relatively simple.

Favorite Grains for Soup
- ❖ Rice
- ❖ Quinoa (high protein)
- ❖ Amaranth (high protein)
- ❖ Barley

Individuals may have differing needs for grain.

Grains have more life force when sprouted and added after soup is cooked (or near end – to warm and soften but keep enzymes alive):
- ❖ Oats
- ❖ Wheat
- ❖ Rye
- ❖ Spelt
- ❖ Triticale
- ❖ Buckwheat

TO SPROUT WHOLE GRAINS

Soak 1-2 c whole grain in water to cover in large wide-mouth jar for 8 hrs. Drain well. Put screen over top with rubber band or ring. Rinse, drain 2 x/day till sprout is length of seed. Serve in soup or salad. Keep in fridge.

MOM'S EASY BARLEY SOUP
~ SUPER IMMUNITY SECRETS ~
TIME: prep ½ hour, cooking 1 ½ hours

Heat big soup pot with 2 quarts water
ADD
- 1 large Onion chopped
- 2-3 1" chunks raw Ginger Root (remove opt)
- 3-4 peeled, sliced Cloves Garlic
- 1 heaping tablespoon Dried Oregano
- 1 heaping teaspoon Curry Powder
- ½ tsp Cumin
- Few needles Rosemary
- ½ tsp med Red Chili powder
- 1 tsp crushed Red Chili
- ½ tsp Sea or Earth Salt
- ½ - 2/3 cup Pearled Barley
- 1/4 cup Amaranth (opt)
- 1-2 large Carrots diced
- 2-3 medium Potatoes – ½" chunks
- 1 large can (28 oz.) diced Tomatoes

Simmer 1 ½ hrs. Last 5-10 minutes add
- 2 cups frozen mixed veggies
- 2-3 T Virgin Olive Oil
- 2 T natural Soy Sauce
- 1 tsp Umeboshi Plum Vinegar

Just before serving stir in
- Medium bunch Parsley chopped fine

Serve with fresh baked bread for the hungry ones; save room for seconds!

A favorite healing meal - adapted from soup Mom used to make. She made it with a meat bone, which you could do depending, on where you are in your dietary transition. However this vegetarian version is so incredibly good once you try it you'll be hooked!

CORN CHOWDER

~ SUPER IMMUNITY SECRETS ~

TIME: prep ½ hr,
cooking ½ hour

**SAUTE´ in
medium soup pot:**
- 3 T Coconut Oil
  or Organic Butter
- 1 large Onion,
  diced
- 3 cloves Garlic,
  peeled and diced
  or crushed
- 6 ears Sweet
  Corn, cut off cob
- 1 bunch Cilantro, chopped
- 1 Sweet Red Pepper, seeded and
  chopped

Add and bring to simmer:
- 3 c Water
- 2 tsp Dill weed
- ½ tsp Coriander
- ½ tsp Red Chili Powder

Blend in blender:
- 3 cups plain Almond, Hazelnut or
  Soy Milk
- 3-4 T flour
- Pinch Earth or Sea Salt

**Add to soup pot, stir and simmer till
slightly thickened.**

Garnish: Chopped Cilantro
SERVE with sliced Tomatoes, Olives,
whole grain or sprouted seed
crackers, mmm...

RICE VEGETABLE

~ SUPER IMMUNITY SECRETS ~
TIME: prep 15 min., cook 1 hour
SHORTCUT – use 10 min. brown rice

Put in 6 quart soup pot and simmer:
- 4 quarts Water
- 1 1/4 cup Organic Brown Rice
- ¼ cup washed Quinoa (opt)
- 1 large can diced Tomatoes w/ juice (or fresh if
  have!)
- 2 large Carrots, diced
- Green onion or leek sliced

Add *Super Immunity Secrets*™ *ingredients*
- 1 large Onion, peeled, diced
- 4 cloves Garlic, peeled, diced
- 2-3 large chunks Ginger root (remove after
  cooking)
- 2 heaping Tablespoons Oregano
- 1 heaping teaspoon Curry powder
- 1 teaspoon Cumin
- ½ teaspoon Green and/or Red Chili powder
- 1 teaspoon crushed Red Chili

Simmer for at least 1 hour.
The rice will thicken up the
soup pot and will absorb a lot
of water, **add additional
water** if needed to keep nice
amount of broth in the pot.

**When done cooking, turn off
heat.**
Remove chunks of ginger if
you wish.
SERVE this hearty, easy to
digest meal with Love and a
spoon.

> *BEANS I know - you're thinking, "Beans have a reputation for being difficult to digest." Beans have been sustenance for primitive cultures for thousands of years; prepared correctly they become quite digestble and an excellent source of vegan protein - this means sprouted and if cooked, slow and long... imagine pot over campfire.*

PROTEIN RICH BEANS

WORLD CUISINE TEACHES US ABOUT MANY VARIETIES OF PEAS AND BEANS

- Pinto
- Anasazi
- Black
- Garbanzo
- Great Northern
- White Kidney
- Red Kidney
- Adzuki
- Mung
- Fava

PEAS

- Lentils
- Red Lentils
- Split / Whole Peas

Beans are Excellent Food

- ✓ Easy on the budget
- ✓ High in vegetable protein
- ✓ Store well
- ✓ Many varieties
- ✓ Easily sprouted & turned into a living food
- ✓ Wide variety around the world

SOAK / SPROUT BEANS & PEAS

Plan ahead, once you work this into your routine, you'll love the results!

➢ Put 1-4 cups whole beans in large wide mouth jar (or bowl) w/ plenty water to cover.

➢ Soak 8-12 hrs (based on size)

➢ After initial soaking, drain well.

➢ Put into soup or crock pot; add water and Super Immunity Secrets™ Ingredients; simmer slowly for several hours.

➢ WOW! Once you taste these you'll never go back to "canned".

➢ Use in soups and other recipes.

➢ Make enough at one time to freeze containers for easy use.

SOURCES: Organically grown beans of many varieties can be found at your natural food market.

We live near an area where beans are commercially grown, and pick up 10# burlap bags of organic pinto and anasazis – to stash

BLACK BEAN or QUICK BLACK BEAN
~ SUPER IMMUNITY SECRETS ~
TIME: prep 15 minutes, cooking 6 hrs
SHORTCUT – with canned beans = 3/4 hr cooking

BLACK BEANS SOAK 12 hours before soup making

➤ **Soak** 4 cups dry Black Beans for 12 hrs to start sprouting process, then simmer in broth below for 6-8 hrs on low heat or in crock pot.

➤ **OR QUICK BLACK BEANS:** use 2 large cans (28 oz) simmer 1 hr.

BROTH with *Super Immunity Ingredients*

- 4 quarts water
- 1 large Onion, peeled, diced
- 4 cloves Garlic, peeled, diced
- 2-3 large chunks Ginger root (remove after cooking)
- 2 heaping Tablespoons Oregano
- 1 heaping teaspoon Curry powder
- 1 teaspoon Cumin
- 1 teaspoon Green and/or Red Chili powder
- 1 teaspoon crushed Red Chili
- ¼ cup chopped Green Chilies (if available)
- Few sprigs Rosemary

Add either the soaked or canned Black Beans (simmer 1 hour w/canned, or 6-8 hrs. over low heat or in crock pot till tender if using fresh soaked beans).

Add more water while cooking to keep up the broth.

When done cooking, turn off heat. Remove chunks of ginger
Blend at least 4 cups of beans and broth in blender and return to pot to make thicker stock; blend about ½ at a time, hold lid with dish towel, slow speed, caution hot.

Then add:
- 1 bunch fresh Cilantro, chopped
- 1 yellow, red or orange Bell Pepper, seeded and chopped
- 1-2 T natural, organic Soy Sauce
- 2-3 T cold pressed, virgin Olive Oil

Stir well and taste. Yum!
Top with Green Onion, thinly sliced. Non-dairy or regular Organic yogurt.

SERVE with Salad of fresh, organic chopped cabbage, diced tomatoes, chopped green onion, dill weed, dressed with fresh lime juice, olive oil and Umeboshi Plum Vinegar.

BLACK BEANS are high in fiber, protein, folic acid, calcium, iron, omega-3 fats, and super-antioxidant flavonoids like those in red grapes and wine.

PINTO BEANS AND RICE
~ SUPER IMMUNITY SECRETS ~
TIME: 12 hrs soak beans, 15 min. prep, 6-8 hrs cooking
SHORTCUT: Use canned beans, 15 min prep, 1 hr. cooking

SOAK 1 1/2 cups dry Pinto Beans for 12 hrs to start sprouting process, then simmer in broth below for 6 hrs on low heat on stove or 8 hrs. in crock pot on low.

OR QUICK PINTO BEANS: If you are pressed for time use 1 large can (15 oz) Pinto Beans with liquid. **Simmer with broth for 1 hr.**

Bring to boil in soup pot:
• 4 quarts water
• 1 large Onion, peeled, diced
• 4 cloves Garlic, peeled, whole
• 2-3 large chunks Ginger root (remove after cooking)

Add *Super Immunity Secrets™ Ingredients*
• 1 T Oregano
• 1 tsp Curry powder
• 1/2 tsp Cumin
• 1 tsp crushed Red Chili
• 1 tsp Red or Green Chili powder
• ½ tsp Sea or Earth Salt
• ½ cup Brown Rice (raw)
• 1 Carrot diced
• Add either the soaked or canned Pinto Beans (above)

SOAKED BEANS – simmer with above ingredients on low 6 hours in soup pot.
CANNED BEANS – simmer with above ingredients on low 1 hour in soup pot

Add more water while cooking if needed to keep broth up. When done cooking, turn off heat. Remove chunks of ginger (opt). Then add:
• 1 bunch fresh Cilantro, chopped
• 1 yellow, red or orange Bell Pepper, seeded and chopped
• 1 T Miso stirred into ¼ cup Water *OR* 2 T natural, organic Soy Sauce
• 3 T cold pressed, virgin Olive Oil or Coconut Oil

Stir well and taste. Mmm!
Top with thinly sliced Green Onion
Optional: organic yogurt or sour cream or non-dairy alternative

LENTIL STEW
~ SUPER IMMUNITY SECRETS ~
TIME: prep 10 minutes, cooking 1 ½ hrs

Opt. Soak 1 c Lentils in water 12 hrs. Drain.
SIMMER in large soup pot

- 3 quarts Water
- 1 cup Lentils (brown).
- ½ cup washed Quinoa
- 1 large Onion, diced
- 4 cloves Garlic, peeled sliced
- 2-1" chunks Ginger Root
- 1 – 2 Carrots, diced
- 1 tsp Cumin
- 1 T Oregano
- 1 tsp Curry Powder
- Few sprigs Rosemary
- 1 tsp favorite Chili Powder
- ¼ tsp Thyme
- 1 tsp Basil (or fresh)

Simmer 1 ½ hrs. till lentils are tender. Add

- 3 T Toasted Sesame Oil or Virgin Olive Oil
- 2-3 T Soy Sauce
- 2-3 T Lemon or Lime Juice
- 1 tsp Umeboshi Plum Vinegar
- 1 bunch Parsley, washed, chopped

Garnish
- Chopped Parsley
- Sliced Green Onion
- Wedge Lemon

SERVE this hearty stew with sliced Cucumbers and sweet peppers.

SPLIT PEA
~ SUPER IMMUNITY SECRETS ~
TIME: prep 10 minutes, cooking 3 hours

SIMMER in large soup pot for 3 hours:

- 4 quarts Water (add more as needed)
- 2 cups Split Peas (may soak in water above overnight)
- 1 large Onion, diced
- 3-4 Cloves Garlic, whole, peeled
- 1 large Carrot, diced (opt)
- 2 T sweet Basil (or ¼ cup fresh)
- 1 T Oregano
- 1 tsp Curry Powder
- 1 tsp Coriander
- 1 T Spearmint or Peppermint
- 1 tsp Dill Weed
- 1 tsp crushed Red Chili
- 1 tsp Green Chili Powder
- ½+ tsp Sea or Earth Salt

Add during last few minutes of cooking:

- 3 T Coconut Oil (or Olive Oil)
- 2 T Soy Sauce
- **Optional** 1 tsp Yellow Curry Paste

Garnish
Chopped Parsley or Cilantro, Sprinkle Dill Weed or Basil Leaf, Wedge Lemon
SERVE this hearty soup with fresh baked crusty bread spread with Coconut Oil or Organic Butter.

IRISH VEGETABLE STEW
~ SUPER IMMUNITY SECRETS™ ~
TIME: prep ½ hr, cooking 1 hour

SAUTE´ in large soup pot:
- 4 T Olive Oil (half coconut oil or butter)
- 1 large Onion, diced
- 4-6 cloves garlic, peeled, diced or crushed
- ½ # Mushrooms, sliced
- 1 sweet Green or Red Pepper, seeded, chopped

Add
- 3 quarts Water
- 2" Ginger Root (opt-remove when done)
- 3-4 Potatoes, cubed
- 2-3 Carrots, sliced
- 2-3 leaves chopped Kale (remove stems)
- 1 can (15 oz) Garbanzo Beans (optional)
- **Frozen** Mixed Veggies 1-2 cups

Add *Super Immunity Secrets™ Ingredients*
- 1 tsp Crushed Red Chili
- ½ tsp Cumin
- ½ tsp Coriander
- 1 tsp Curry Powder
- ½ tsp Earth or Sea Salt
- 1 T Oregano
- ¼ tsp Thyme
- 1 tsp Dill Weed

When potatoes are tender, blend:
- 1 cup Water or Broth
- 6 T flour (whole wheat)
- 2 T Miso (or 3 T Soy Sauce)
- 1 tsp Umeboshi Plum Vinegar

Stir into stew and simmer till thickened.

Add
- 1 bunch washed, chopped Parsley

Ladle into mugs or bowls. Serve with crusty bread, and Rice, Soy or Organic Cheddar cheese.

STONE SOUP
~ SUPER IMMUNITY SOUP ~
TIME: whatever you want

FOLLOW RECIPE below ~
Use good ingredients. Give thanks!
Enjoy with Friends!

HAVE YOU HAD STONE SOUP?

Once upon a time, long long ago, a poor old woman stood on a street corner. She huddled close to the small fire crackling beneath her big cooking pot full of water. The big black pot was her most prized possession because it carried with it so many good memories.

She invited passersby to come to dinner; she said, "We'll have Stone Soup, all you need to bring is a bowl, a spoon and one ingredient..."

The townfolk came back one by one as the day faded... one brought a potato, another a carrot; one an onion, another a bulb of garlic; one person brought herbs from a pot on the windowsill, another a small handful of beans for they swell when they cook; one brought barley grown in a field nearby, another a basket of garden vegetables; strangers from faraway brought handfuls of rice, quinoa and amaranth; one brought a pinch of salt, another offered a small flask of oil.

The pot was so full it bubbled over; the aroma drew the guests closer and closer, talking of families and their day. A young maid from the village brought crusts of bread from the bakery, and set them in a pan next to the fire to warm. It smelled so good her guests finally couldn't wait any longer for the old woman to fill their bowls with her incredible Stone Soup.

Conversation lulled and all that could be heard was ...mmmm... as they enjoyed Stone Soup and dipping crusts of bread, as much or more than any meal they had ever had; *and* when their bowls were empty there was enough left to fill them again. The little old lady was very happy to share her dinner, and she slept peacefully that night, dreaming of other days of Stone Soup.

The MORAL OF THE STORY is you can make Stone Soup out of almost anything, make a lot with a little, invite your friends and don't do it all yourself – how with just a little bit of artistry, a stone and a pot of water, you can have an amazing meal!

Chapter 3:
Super Immunity Salads and Light Fare

A SALAD A DAY KEEPS THE DOCTOR AWAY!

Sweet, juicy fresh and raw organic fruits and vegetables have *got to be* the very best food on the planet!

I'm so excited when fresh fruits and veggies come into season ~ sweet juicy watermelon, cantaloupe, apricots, apples, peaches, tomatoes, cucumbers, peppers, peas, pomegranates, mango, papaya, corn, squash, garden fresh herbs and more!!!

If you aren't hooked on the Salad Habit yet it's time to start! Think of Salad as the Main Dish rather than a side dish... A big bowl of fresh crisp veggies with lettuce, sprouts and virgin olive oil, lime juice and herbs is so good ~ and good for ya!

Be sure to learn about *Super Immunity* Ingredients in Chapter 2, that are also used with recipes in this chapter.

...And then fresh luscious fruit, fruit salads and shakes for breakfast with green powder for protein ~ what else is there? This is truly the exotic healthy lifestyle!

Did you know that a dollar spent at a local business turns over 7 times in your community, while the same dollar spent in a box store or chain turns over only 2.5 times? *Learn more at* <u>www.organicconsumers.org</u>

GROW IT! BUY LOCAL ORGANIC OR HAVE YOUR OWN GARDEN!!!

Wherever you live, there is most likely locally grown produce available at a farmers' market, natural foods co-op, share-gardens, organic grower or rancher. Nose around your area and see what you can find.

We have so many out of season foods shipped to our supermarkets. This food is less fresh, costs us and the environment more in fuel to ship and store, and does not have the vitality to nourish us as well as locally grown organic.

Once you taste and experience locally grown food, you'll look for it with excitement every growing season and never go back. You'll encourage local food security and support your local economy by knowing your growers.

VOTE FOR THE FUTURE WITH YOUR FORK!

Pesticides and fossil fuels from industrial agriculture put more carbon into the atmosphere. Organically grown food holds carbon dioxide in the soil and contributes to a healthier ecosystem.

Choose organic. Pay a little extra now or pay later in health and environmental costs. Organic global agriculture, reduces our carbon footprint by 40%!

Experiment with a small garden, or grow food in pots - a great way for big and little kids to learn where food comes from. Visit virtualearthvillage.com for great ideas on how to fill your yard with fun and food.

TOSSIN' A SALAD TO MAKE YOUR DAY COMPLETE

~ SUPER IMMUNITY SECRETS™ ~
TIME: 10 minutes

BE CREATIVE - TEAR, CUT, SNIP - MAKE IT TASTY AND FUN

> **Lettuces:** romaine, bibb, leaf, escarole, endive, spring greens
> **Herbs:** fresh/dry basil, oregano, thyme, rosemary, dill, cilantro, parsley, borage
> **Veggies:** cucumber, tomato, peas, mushrooms, peppers, red/purple cabbage, bok choy, green/wax beans, summer squash, celery, fennel, raw corn cut off cob
> **Greens:** arugula, spinach, kale; **Wild:** dandelion, purslane, lambsquarter
> **Sprouts:** alfalfa, clover, mung, aduki, pea, lentil, wheat, rye, broccoli
> **Flowers:** nasturtium, violet, borage,
> **Root:** grated or chopped - beet, carrot, jicama, sunchoke, parsnip, turnip
> **Savory:** onion, scallions, garlic, chives, ginger, chili, jalapeno, hot peppers
> **Hearty:** avocado, nuts, seeds, seed cheese, organic cheese or substitute, tofu
> **Cooked:** beans (black/garbanzo/northern/kidney), rice, quinoa

And more! See next page for how to Dress your Salad. Once you become a Creative Salad Maker - you'll avoid all boring   salads from this day forth and Crave Your Own!

DRESSING YOUR SALAD

Adopt a new concept in "salad dressing" - a good opportunity to have premium raw ingredients as flavorful additions to your salad. If using bottled dressing, find a light, natural brand. Read labels and you'll find those that have olive oil, are often cut with canola or soy oil and have lots of vinegar (*a powerful preservative that inhibits digestion*) preferably used in moderation. Experiment with the recipes below and discover your own favorites using ingredients to feed and nourish.

LIGHT OLIVE OIL AND HERB DRESSING
~ SUPER IMMUNITY SECRETS ~
TIME: 5 minutes

Drizzle any combo of the following ingredients over a salad or make your own bottle:

- Olive Oil - extra virgin, cold pressed (primary)
- Sesame, Flaxseed, Hemp, Almond or Walnut oil (in smaller quantities)
- Generous Herbs fresh or dry: Oregano, Dill, Rosemary, Thyme,Cilantro, Parsley
- Nama Shoyu (raw soy sauce)
- Umeboshi Plum vinegar (alkalizing)
- Fresh Lemon or Lime juice
- Raw Ginger root, blend with water in blender, strain (use the liquid)
- Extra water can be added if making a jar to shake

CREAMY SEED DRESSING OR DIP (oil free)
~ SUPER IMMUNITY SECRETS ~
TIME: 10 minutes

Use a combination seeds or nuts with a sunflower seed base:
sunflower, sesame, pumpkin, almond, walnut, pecan, brazil, hemp, macadamia.

Soak 4 hours to start sprouting, or use without soaking (thicker)

Blend together in blender till creamy:
- 1/2 cup nuts or seeds (described above) with 1 cup water
- Generous Herbs dry: Oregano, Dill, Rosemary, Thyme, Cilantro
- Pinch Curry or Chili powder
- 1 tsp Nama Shoyu (raw soy sauce)
- Dash Umeboshi Plum vinegar (alkalizing)
- 1 T Fresh Lemon or Lime juice
- 2 T Raw Ginger root, blend with water, strain (use liquid)

Serve: over salad, or make thicker to serve as a dip.

WHY ARE SPROUTS GOOD FOR US? / SPROUT FOR LIFE

Sprouts are the first 7 days of growth of a plant or seed.

During this time the plant is growing at a rapid rate with amazing life force All its focus is on growing a plant to produce a seed, to generate new life. These plant cells have a high concentration of living enzymes - and when we eat them, they bring life force and regenerative qualities to our bodies.

Dr. Edward Howell did some of the most dedicated research and writing on enzymes available today. He recognized enzymes as a very unique and important component in our food.

"Enzymes may be the key factor in preventing chronic disease and extending the human lifespan."

Born in 1898 Dr. Howell was a practicing physician until 1970, and to this day his work is recognized as some of the foremost research in this field, demonstrating that enzymes assist with digestion, carrying away of waste, and cleansing of cells - all critical to health. Dr. Howell's work is carried on by co-author Don Weaver. Download a free pdf of their exciting work, The Survival of Civilization at http://www.remineralize.org/don/synopsis01.html

GROW YOUR OWN SPROUTS - SPROUT FOR LIFE

Sprouting is easy - use a wide mouth Mason jar with ring lid and a piece of screen on top. Soak seeds in jar in plenty of water to cover for 4-8 hrs depending on size of seed. After soaking, turn upside down to drain in dish drainer. Keep out of direct sun; rinse and drain 2x/day till sprout is desired length or at least length of the seed. Serve on salads, make breads, add to soup. Sprouts are a very inexpensive life-giving food.

CAUTION: NEVER buy agricultural seeds (often treated w/chemical poisons) - use seeds "for sprouting" from a reliable natural food supplier.

TABOULI - Middle Eastern Salad
~ SUPER IMMUNITY SECRETS ~
TIME: 15 minutes + prepare grain

Use ONE of the following Grains:

1. BULGAR WHEAT: 3/4 cup bulgar wheat: soak 3-4 hrs in plenty of water to cover; drain off water, squeeze out excess water. *(grain traditionally used)*

2. WHOLE GRAIN CRACKED WHEAT: Soak 3/4 cup cracked wheat in plenty of water to cover for 12 hours. Drain, squeeze out excess water.

3. SPROUTED WHEAT: Soak 1/2 cup whole grain winter wheat in jar with plenty of water 8 hours; drain, rinse 2 x / day for 2 days; run through food processor with blade to grind up a bit or use whole.

4. QUINOA: (High protein Peruvian grain). Soak 3/4 cup quinoa for 1/2 hr in cool water or for 5 min. with hot water, drain in strainer and rinse a couple of times to remove outer coating of saponin which is a little bitter. Put quinoa in small saucepan with 1 1/4 cups water & pinch salt; simmer 15 minutes covered; turn heat off and let sit covered for 5 more minutes. Cool. (Also experiment w/sprouting quinoa).

Put grain of choice in large bowl.

Add the following and toss together well:
- 1-2 large bunches Parsley, washed, stemmed, chopped fine by hand or food processor
- 3-4 scallions sliced thin
- 2-3 tomatoes diced fine
- 2 T dry or 1/4 cup fresh spearmint or peppermint
- 1 tsp Oregano or Thyme
- 1/2 cup fresh or frozen peas (thawed), opt.
- 1/2 finely diced cucumber, opt.
- 1/4 c Olive Oil
- 1/4 c Lemon or Lime juice
- 1 T Nama Shoyu (raw soy sauce)
- Earth or Sea Salt to taste

Serve: This hearty salad can comprise a meal with pita bread, side dish or wrap.

Variations: Traditional Tabouli is based on seasonal nutritional needs and produce availability. Experiment!

CAN'T BEAT BEETS!

RAW BEET SALAD
~ SUPER IMMUNITY SECRETS ~
TIME: 15 minutes

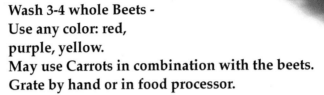

Wash 3-4 whole Beets -
Use any color: red,
purple, yellow.
May use Carrots in combination with the beets.
Grate by hand or in food processor.

Dress with:
- Fresh Lemon or Lime juice
- Olive oil
- Umeboshi Plum vinegar
- Dill weed, cilantro or parsley

Beets have long been used as a cleanser for liver and gall bladder in combination with lemon juice and olive oil. This is a delightful crunchy, sweet fresh salad.

STEAMED BEET SALAD
~ SUPER IMMUNITY SECRETS ~
TIME: 1/2 hour pre + 15 minutes

Wash 3-4 large beets. Cut into 1/2" cubes.
Put in saucepan with about 1" water, cover and steam over medium heat till tender but firm, cool.
Put beets in bowl, add and toss:
- 1/2 cup Walnut pieces
- 2-3 Scallions sliced
- 2 cloves minced Garlic
- 1/2 cup chopped Parsley
- 2-3 T Olive Oil
- 1 T Lemon juice
- 1 T Nama Shoyu (raw soy sauce)
- Dill weed

Serve as side dish or lunch; this is so good there won't be much leftover.

BUY ORGANIC: Beets are one of the foods commonly genetically modified. For full natural nutrition buy organic and heirloom when possible.

NOTE: Eating beets can turn elimination red - this is normal, not to worry about.

MORE SALAD IDEAS: HEARTY, FUN & NUTRITIOUS

Salad Additions

TIME: 10 minutes

Awesome salad ideas below -

✓**healthy vegetarian protein**

✓**fat burning fats & carbs**

✓**amazing taste**

✓**fill you up**

✓**satisfying**

✓**sustaining**

ADD FAVORITES TO SALADS FOR MORE PROTEIN TO MAKE A HEARTY MEAL

- NUTS - Walnuts, Almonds, Pecans (raw - any nut/ soaked for better digestion)
- EGGS - Hard Boiled Eggs (organic, free range)
- CHEESE - non dairy or organic dairy
- TOFU - Tofu, cubed or crumbled
- PEAS - Peas in the pod, edamame
- BEANS - Garbanzos, Navy, Black, Great Northern, Pinto, Kidney, Black Eyed Peas (canned, sprouted or soaked & slow cooked)

- ESSENTIAL OILS - Avocado, Olives, Hemp Seed
- SEEDS - Pumpkin, Sesame or Sunflower Seeds (raw, soaked or dehydrated w/ seasoning)
- GRAIN - such as Rice or Quinoa, cooked, cooled
- SEED CHEESE - raw seeds blended, seasoned and cultured
- FUNGI / FLOWERS - Mushrooms, Flowers
- VEGGIES Grilled, baked or stir-fried Veggies and Root Veggies

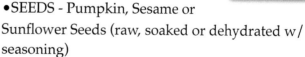
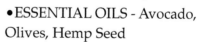

PASTA SALAD POSSIBILITIES

Pasta Salad Possibilities are endless.

Inexpensive and readily available, pasta comes in a zillion varieties. Grab spirals for the kids or handmade gourmet pasta for a nice dinner.

Use the ordinary familiar white, or experiment with healthy blends made from whole grains and legumes.

Recipes below have more veggies than pasta - a new adventure in taste and lighter eating - leave out heavy cream and overcooked tomato sauce. You might eventually leave pasta behind, but it offers a simple healthy food choice for kids, athletes, hard workin' folks and the whole family, friends or a party.

PASTA ADDITIONS
~ SUPER IMMUNITY SECRETS ~
TIME: 30 + 10 minutes

CHOOSE A PASTA AND USE WITH RECIPES BELOW

COOK PASTA according to directions on package. Rinse with cool water. Drain in colander. Return to pot.

SEASON PASTA - (toss gently in pot while warm)
- Generous Olive Oil
- Sprinkle Earth or Sea Salt
- Sprinkled crushed Red or Black Pepper
- 1-2 T Oregano dried or fresh snipped
- Dash of Soy Sauce or Nama Shoyu (raw)

ADD ONE OF THESE COMBINATIONS TO COOKED/ SEASONED PASTA (above)

- Snipped fresh Basil leaves, Cherry Tomatoes, crumbled Feta or Tofu, Olives
- Grilled or steamed veggies: Zucchini, Asparagus, Green Beans, Peppers, Tomatoes
- Add Spirals or Tubes to Tossed Salad
- Asparagus, Snap Peas, Artichoke Hearts
- Thinly sliced steamed Zucchini, Parmesan Cheese, fresh Basil

ELEGANT HEALTHY PASTA DINNERS

Cook and Season Pasta of choice as directed on previous page. Toss or top with either Spinach or Pesto.

These extra-special recipes for Spinach and Pesto are full of concentrated nutrients for cleansing, healing and vitality. They are great addition to either a routine healthy menu or for a nice candlelight dinner.

SAVORY SPINACH - PASTA DINNER
~ SUPER IMMUNITY SECRETS ~
TIME: 30 + 10 minutes

COOK PASTA according to directions on package. Rinse with cool water. Drain in colander. Return to pot. Mix with seasonings below and toss gently in pot while warm.
- Generous Olive Oil
- Sprinkle Earth or Sea Salt
- Sprinkled crushed Red or Black Pepper
- 1-2 T Oregano dried or fresh snipped
- Dash of Soy Sauce or Nama Shoyu (raw)

Warm in large skillet on medium heat:
- 2-3 T Olive Oil
- 4-5 cloves Garlic sliced with skin on
- 2-3 sliced Scallions (opt)
- 6-8 sliced mushrooms
- 1-2 washed bunches Spinach (chop lightly)
- 1-2 T dried Oregano or Dill (or fresh)
- Dash Soy Sauce
- Dash Umeboshi Plum Vinegar
- 1/2 cup Red Wine

Cover. Steam just 1-2 minutes till spinach is barely wilted.

Serve immediately on top of pasta.

Optional - if still eating cheese sprinkle with parmesan or feta otherwise enjoy vegan-style. A great replacement for cheese is Flaked Nutritional Yeast.

NOTE: This is a great way to offer kids an opportunity to like spinach (leave out the wine).

PESTO IS FOR LOVERS

Basil grows abundantly in warm climates such as Italy - not so well in cold country. Basil must be fresh for pesto (dried just won't do). However a pesto-look-alike can also be made with other fresh herbs such as cilantro, and is quite delightful. Basil has an almost intoxicating aroma giving it the reputation for being aphrodisiac, and the saying "pesto is for lovers" inspires us to get out the candles and enjoy...

PESTO (Pasta Dinner or Spread)
~ SUPER IMMUNITY SECRETS ~
TIME: 1 hour (cook pasta & make pesto)

Chop in food processor with blade:

- 1 bunch Parsley, washed, broken, no stems
- 2 cups fresh Basil leaves
- 3-5 cloves Garlic (to taste)
- 3/4 cup Pine Nuts or Walnuts
- 1/4 tsp Sea or Earth Salt
- NOTE: traditional pesto contains Parmesan and/or Romano cheese - if you're still eating dairy, add 1/4-1/3 cup either or both (optional)

Then pour in slowly through hole in top while blending:
- 1/2 - 1 cup Olive Oil

Run food processor 2-3 minutes till smooth consistency

Serve: Toss with Pasta to lightly coat

Other Ways to Serve Pesto:
- Dip with crackers and/or veggies
- Vegetarian or raw Pizza topping w/ veggies
- Replace basil with Cilantro - (helps detoxify mercury out of the body)
- Eat it by the spoonful
- Add to salad dressing recipe
- On crusty bread with a glass of wine...

ONCE UPON A TIME... in the southern clime of North Carolina, there grew gigantic basil plants so big that a pesto party became the fine tradition every fall.

With bread, wine, olive oil and pine nuts, friends arrived from far and near to make unique batches of pesto, taste tested and in the freezer for winter.

These days basil doesn't grow so big in the chilly Rockies - though we're getting greenhouse smart...with a little basil plant in a sunny window dreaming of a pesto party.

EASY & FUN GOURMET SALADS

SPINACH SALAD
~ SUPER IMMUNITY SECRETS ~
TIME: 15 minutes

Carefully wash and rinse large bunch Spinach - shake dry.

Put in large bowl with:
- Thinly sliced Purple Onions
- Mandarin Orange slices
- Raw or toasted Sunflower Seeds
- Peas (fresh or frozen thawed)

Dressing:
Make very thin version of *Creamy Sunflower Seed Dressing*. (page 41)
Toss with ingredients in bowl and serve.

SPRING GREENS SALAD
~ SUPER IMMUNITY SECRETS ~
TIME: 10 minutes

Place Spring Greens **on individual salad plate or bowl:**

Top with:
- Tomatoes
- Walnuts or Pecans
- Crushed Oregano, Dill or Thyme
- Organic cheese or cheese substitute, tofu, crumbled feta or seed cheese

Dressing: Drizzle with *Light Olive Oil & Herb Dressing* **(page 41)**

HEIRLOOM TOMATO & HERB SALAD
~ SUPER IMMUNITY SECRETS ~
TIME: 10 minutes

Toss gently together in salad bowl:
- Handfuls of fresh garden herbs snipped with scissors - Basil, Dill, Oregano, Rosemary, Thyme
- Cubed Heirloom Tomatoes (or any good fresh juicy sweet organic tomatoes)
- Thinly sliced Scallions or Purple Onion
- Cubes of Tofu or Organic Cheese
- Dash crushed or ground Red Chili
- *Light Olive Oil & Herb Dressing (page 41)*

GREEK SALAD
~ SUPER IMMUNITY SECRETS ~
TIME: 15 minutes

Fill individual salad bowls with bed of Lettuce:
Romaine, Endive, Spring Greens (or whatever you have)

Layer on top any combination of:
• Cubed or sliced ripe Tomatoes or Cherry Tomatoes
• Sliced and separated Purple Onion
• Sliced or cubed Cucumber (wash, don't peel)
• Black or Green Olives (preferably traditional Greek)

• Crushed Oregano (generous)
• Crushed Red Pepper (pinch)
• Fresh Dill Weed (opt.)
  • Crumble Feta Cheese or Tofu on top

Dressing - Shake or beat together and Pour over salad:

• Olive Oil - 2 parts
• Balsamic Vinegar - 2 parts
• Fresh Lemon Juice - 1 part

Enjoy with crusty whole grain bread or sprouted Essene bread or crackers.

SUSTAINING BEAN SALADS

GARBANZO SALAD
~ SUPER IMMUNITY SECRETS ~
TIME: 10 minutes

Toss gently together in large bowl:

- 2 cans Garbanzo Beans (or Chick Peas) drained (or 3 cups Sprouted or Precooked)
- Thinly sliced Scallions or Purple Onions
- 1/2 cup finely chopped washed Parsley
- 1/2 cup finely chopped washed Cilantro
- Crushed Oregano
- Pinch crushed Red Pepper or Black
- 1/2 tsp Curry Powder
- 1 Lemon or Lime juiced
- Dash Umeboshi Plum Vinegar (opt.)
- 1 T Soy Sauce
- 2-3 T Olive Oil

Serve with pita bread as a meal or side w/ tossed salad.

Lentils and garbanzos are ancient foods - versatile and high in protein.

Depending on where you are in *your* dietary transition - you may prefer them cooked, or you may like the crisp crunch of them sprouted.

Easy to sprout - just soak 8-12 hrs. and rinse 2x/day for 1-2 days. Makes them easier to digest (*i.e.: no gas*) and makes them a Living Food with lots of enzymes and life force.

Either way they are an excellent food for weight loss, strength and endurance.

LENTIL SALAD - SPROUTED OR COOKED
~ SUPER IMMUNITY SECRETS ~
TIME: 2-3 days + 30 minutes

Soak 1 cup Lentils overnight in water to cover.
Drain. Rinse 2x/day for 1 day for cooked salad, for 2 days for raw salad.

COOKED LENTIL SALAD
Saute on med heat 7-8 minutes until tender but firm:
- 2T Olive Oil
- 3 cloves Garlic sliced (not peeled)
- 1 large onion, diced
- 1/2 tsp Cumin
- 1/4 tsp Curry Powder
- Pinch crushed Red Pepper
- Lentils sprouted for 1 day (above)
- 1 T Soy Sauce

Cool. Then add:
- Diced sweet Red Pepper, Tomato, Cucumber,
- Grated Carrot
- Sunflower Seeds or Pine Nuts
- Drizzle Olive Oil
- Dash Umeboshi Plum vinegar or Lemon or Lime juice

RAW LENTIL SALAD
Soak Lentils and Sprout 2 days (described above).

Toss in salad bowl with:
- Raw chopped Green Beans or Asparagus (seasonal)
- Diced Tomato, Cucumber, Sweet Pepper
- Sliced Scallions
- Finely chopped Parsley
- Fresh or crushed Oregano (generous)
- Crushed or ground Red Chili
- 1/2 tsp Curry Powder
- 1/4 tsp Cumin
- 2 T Olive Oil
- Juice of 1/2 Lemon or Lime
- Dash Nama Shoyu (raw) Soy Sauce

Serve with sprouted grain Essene bread or crackers.

DIPS AND SPREADS

HUMMUS
popular Middle Eastern garbanzo dip
~ SUPER IMMUNITY SECRETS ~
TIME: 15 minutes (+ 2 days if you sprout)

Put in blender or food processor (with blade) and run till smooth:
- 1 can Garbanzos with liquid (or your own pre-cooked)
- 4T Sesame Tahini (sesame butter)
- Juice of 1 Lemon (or lime)
- 1/4 tsp Earth or Sea Salt

Use rubber spatula and scrape into bowl.

Garnish: Drizzle with a little Olive Oil, sprinkle with Paprika

Serve:
- Dip with Veggies
- Appetizer with Crackers
- Spread for sandwich or roll-up

RAW HUMMUS: Soak dry garbanzo beans 12 hours and sprout 2 days; use raw sesame tahini - available in jar or make your own; add lemon juice, salt and garnish as directed above. The raw garbanzo sprouts are a cultivated taste
- but if you're going raw it's a great dip or spread.

BABAGANOUSH
popular Middle Eastern eggplant dip
~ SUPER IMMUNITY SECRETS ~
TIME: 1/2 hr prep + 15 minutes

Bake at 425° on dry baking sheet for 30 minutes or till soft: 2 large Eggplants

When cool, scrape inside of eggplants (I often use skin also - not traditional) into blender and add:

- 3 T Sesame Tahini,
- 1/4 tsp salt,
- 1 Lemon juiced (or lime)

Use rubber spatula and scrape into bowl.

Garnish: drizzle with Olive Oil & sprinkle Paprika or Chili Powder

Serve:
Dip with Veggies, Appetizer with Crackers
Spread for sandwich or roll-up

GRILLED VEGGIES
~ SUPER IMMUNITY SECRETS~
TIME: 10-15 minutes

Prepare any of the following veggies (no need to peel) into slices or chunks and put them on the grill. Grill to perfection and serve as main entrée or side dish.

- Zucchini
- Eggplant
- Potatoes
- Sweet Potato, Yam
- Peppers
- Onions
- Asparagus
- Green Beans
- Tomatoes
- Corn

Blend in blender for marinade:

- Olive Oil, Soy Sauce, small amount of water to thin, squeeze lemon juice
- Oregano, Dill, Basil, Rosemary, Thyme
- Curry Powder, crushed Chili, Cumin, pinch salt
  - Pressed Garlic
  - Touch of Honey (opt)

Toss vegetables in bowl with marinade, turn occasionally to re-coat, then grill.

NOTE: A special grill screen is available at kitchen stores to hold the veggies on grill.

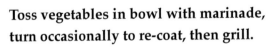

VEGGIE WRAPS
TIME: 10-15 minutes

Keep a variety of 10" - 12" Tortillas or Wraps on hand - many kinds available today - veggie & herb, sprouted, spelt or multi-grain.

A wrap is a great "fast food" and easy to take along for lunch or snack. Be creative, find out what your family likes, and put a wrap in their hand as they walk out the door. They'll appreciate having something healthy to eat.

ART OF ROLLING A WRAP -
1. Put spread on entire wrap
2. Veggie mixture put mound in middle crossways
3. Fold wrap in from sides 2"
4. Roll up from bottom - snug
5. Wrap in paper towel and or plastic wrap
6. Go to a restaurant where they make wraps. Watch!

FILLING A WRAP or make up your own

1. Spread with **Nut Butter** (peanuts are a legume not a nut - they are cheap food but can have mold and cause food allergies). A better choice is Almond Butter or other nut butters. Keep them on hand - very nutritious. (raw is best)

2. **Hummus or Babaganoush or Pesto** - spread on wrap, then add mound of minced **Veggies** such as tomato, cabbage, cucumber, lettuce, sprouts, avocado, olive, grated carrots or beets

3. **Grilled or stir-fried Veggies** such as zucchini, mushrooms, onion, garlic

4. **Tabouli** & leaf lettuce, with Hummus (opt)

5. **Breakfast burrito** home fries, eggs or tofu, cheese or cheese substitute, green chili, salsa, hot sause

6. **Beans & Rice** w/Salsa

7. **Black Beans** with grilled Peppers and Onions

8. **Tofu or Egg Salad**, lettuce, tomatoes

SOME KINDA SANDWICH
~ SUPER IMMUNITY SECRETS ~
TIME: 10-15 minutes

NOTE ON BREAD
With the low carb craze bread is a bad word in many households; however whole grains are an excellent inexpensive healthy food to enjoy in Moderation.

Rule # 1 Get rid of the whites (white flour / white sugar - *read the label*)

Rule #2 Go for a hearty crusty coarse multigrain

Rule #3 Discover Essene bread made from 100% sprouted grains / no flour (learn to make it and crackers)

Try out these sandwiches or make up your own:
1. Lettuce, tomato, cucumber, sprouts w/ *Sunflower Dressing (page 41)*
2. Essene bread with *Pesto*, lettuce, tomato, sprouts (see page 56 for Pesto dressing)
3. Veggie burger with lettuce, onion, tomato, mustard
4. Pickles, lettuce, tomato, tofu or cheese, fresh herbs, hummus or babaganoush
5. Almond butter, sliced apples
6. Tofu or egg salad, lettuce, tomato

RICE IS NICE
TIME: 1 hour

An excellent grain to add heartiness to meals, rice is non allergenic, with many varieties to choose from, as jasmine, short and long grain, basmati. (For a quick meal use 10 minute rice).

Rice is a staple for over half the world's population and whole or unrefined is nutrient-packed, as in "brown" rice. A friend from the Philippines tells the story of seed companies pushing them to use genetically modified rice. The growers knew the westerners wouldn't walk into the rice paddies. They planted the new seed in the front where it was visible, and their old heirloom varieties in the back for their own consumption (how wise)!

To Cook Brown Rice:

Put 1 part brown rice and 2.5 parts water into pot with a pinch of salt. Bring to boil. Cook covered on low heat for 50 minutes. Turn off heat and keep covered for 10 more minutes. Then remove cover and serve. Cooking time may vary slightly depending upon variety of rice.

Variation: Measure dry jasmine or lighter rice into saucepan with 1-2 tablespoons butter or olive oil and 1/2-1 teaspoon curry powder, stir over medium heat till golden. Then add 2 parts water to 1 part rice. Cover, simmer over low heat about 35 minutes, let sit 10 minutes more to steam without removing cover. Then serve.

Serve: Rice is a wonderful staple, served with veggies or beans, or cold on a salad.

QUINOA - GREAT ALTERNATIVE TO RICE

Quinoa is a tasty ancient grain from South America, quick cooking with complete vegetarian protein! Before cooking rinse well in several changes of cool water to remove natural bitter residue, drain in strainer.

To cook: Bring 2 cups water, 1 cup quinoa and 1/4 tsp salt to simmer in small saucepan. Turn heat to low; simmer 5 minutes covered. Then turn heat off and let sit another 5 minutes - till ready to serve.

Serve: cold on salad, warm with veggies, as breakfast with raisins; also use in *Tabouli* (page 43) as a replacement for bulgar wheat.

SKILLET POTATOES
~ SUPER IMMUNITY SECRETS~
TIME: 35-40 minutes

Put into skillet on medium heat in this order:
- 2-3 T Olive Oil
- 4-5 Cloves Garlic sliced (not peeled)
- 1 Onion, diced (opt)
- 1/2 Sweet Pepper, diced (opt)
- 6-7 medium sized Potatoes, washed, cut in 1/2" cubes
- 1-2 tsp Dill Weed
- 1/2 tsp Curry Powder
- 1/4 tsp crushed Chili or powder
- 2-3 T Soy Sauce
- dash Umeboshi Plum Vinegar

Turn with spatula and cover. Allow to cook in their own steam, turn occasionally, and keep cover on. Serve with salsa, toast, scrambled eggs or tofu or in a wrap.

HERBED POTATO ROUNDS
"instead of potato chips"
~ SUPER IMMUNITY SECRETS ~
TIME: 35-40 minutes

Preheat oven to 400° - and get ready for this favorite treat!

Cut into 1/3" thick slices (don't peel):
- washed Potatoes
- washed Sweet Potatoes or Yams

Rub Olive Oil lightly on baking sheet; lay potato slices on it as closely as possible

Sprinkle with:
- Dill weed (lots)
- mild Chili powder (generous)
- a touch of salt
- sprinkle soy sauce (with thumb over top of bottle)

Bake about 30 minutes or until potatoes are tender. Serve in basket or bowl with salsa. Great party treat - they will disappear!!!

CABBAGE SAUTÉ
~ SUPER IMMUNITY SECRETS ~
TIME: 25 minutes

Layer in large skillet on medium heat:

- 2-3 T Olive Oil
- 3-4 Cloves Garlic sliced (do no peel)
- 3-4 Scallions sliced
- 1/2 head Cabbage sliced thin with sharp knife or shred in food processor
- 2 tsp Oregano
- 1/2 tsp crushed Chili
- 1/2 tsp Curry Powder
- 1-2 T Soy Sauce or Nama Shoyu (raw)
- dash Umeboshi Plum Vinegar

Cover and allow to steam in its own moisture, stirring occasionally, covered till cabbage is tender but firm.

Serve as a meal or with rice and salad.

NOTE: Cabbage and other members of the brassica family such as kale, broccoli and brussels sprouts demonstrate potent anti-cancer properties in clinical studies; excellent to include regularly in a healthy dietary routine. Cabbage family vegetables can also reduce thyroid function, so for those with this issue, use less often.

VARIATION
Sauté other veggies of choice individually or together. Experiment with kale, broccoli, zucchini, mushrooms, summer squash, green beans, asparagus, corn, tomatoes in similar manner, vary seasonings.

EATING OUT - A FOREIGN AFFAIR

These days we don't want to (or can't) prepare all meals at home, as social contact and interesting diversity of life is enhanced by the enjoyment of eating out.

Cuisines from cultures that go back hundreds, or even thousands of years, rooted in simple living with agricultural roots, offer fantastic and delicious combinations of vegetables, seasonings, grains and beans. Readily available choices include Chinese, Japanese, Asian, Mexican, Middle Eastern, Italian and even Ethiopian.

Seek out Mexican restaurants that use all fresh ingredients and offer vegetarian bean preparations without lard; at Chinese and Asian always request no MSG.

If you're lucky enough to have a great raw or natural foods restaurant or deli near where you live, go there for both ideas and great food. Otherwise, get to know cross-cultural restaurants offering healthiest food prep choices; or contemporary restaurants serving fresh salads and vegetables.

For "fast food" a sandwich shop offering wraps or multigrain bread with fresh veggies or salad, is a better choice than conventional fast food or fried. Continuing on your path of well-being, look for restaurants that match your choice of quality, and don't be afraid to ask for what you want that might be a deviation from the menu - often you'll get a *yes*!

FRESH AND RAW BREAKFAST AND SNACK IDEAS

BUGS BUNNY CARROT JUICE
~ SUPER IMMUNITY SECRETS ~
TIME: 15 minutes

Get out your juicer and get juiced!
Juice a cupful of carrot juice - preferably organic. Put in jar or cup with more space; add 1/4 cup or so Almond or Hazelnut milk. Drink slowly and savor...mmm...

This can be a *meal* such as breakfast or lunch. It will depend on where you are in your dietary transition how sustaining it is. As we eat lighter foods and the cells get cleaned out, the body can take in its nutrition in a finer way.

I had a Bugs Bunny in Maui years ago, but made with carrot juice and ice cream! I came home and made up this version - with no guilt and years of enjoyment!

WHAT IS WHEATGRASS?
~ SUPER IMMUNITY SECRETS ~
TIME: days + 15 minutes

Wheatgrass is the first 7 days of growth of the wheat plant.

HOW TO GROW Soak whole grain winter wheat for 8 hours, rinse and drain for 2 days, until the sprout is the length of the grain. Then spread the sprouted seeds on a tray of dirt. Water, cover and allow to grow. Once the root has gone into the soil, uncover the tray, water, and in 5-7 days you'll have 6-7" tall wheatgrass! Cut the grass before it splits to send out the stalk to grow seeds, so powerful nutrients are in the grass itself.

HOW TO USE In order to extract the juice from the wheatgrass you'll need either an old fashioned hand meat grinder or an actual wheatgrass juicer - hand or electric.

Once the juice is extracted drink shots of it, or use in many other ways. **Caution:** wheatgrass will burn out a regular veggie juicer.

ALTERNATE METHOD Put several cups water in a blender with handfuls of wheatgrass. Blend, strain, drink.

WHEATGRASS TABLETS are an excellent whole superfood supplement. They have proven to improve cancer conditions and diabetes.

TRUE STORY *When Dr. Ann Wigmore's grandmother's village was bombed in WWI in Poland, she hid in the fields and lived on grass for a year! Everything healed, including her teeth; she took in soldiers with gangrenous wounds, saving their lives with wheatgrass poultices, juice and goats' milk.*

When Dr. Ann discovered she had cancer at age 50, she turned to memories of her grandmother and used wheatgrass to heal. She then gave wheatgrass juice to invalids in Boston with such great results she founded The Hippocrates Health Institute, popularizing wheatgrass and living foods!

Breakfast is an important meal. Be creative and experiment using fresh wholesome organic fruits, nuts, seeds and milk alternatives such as Almond. Depending on your caloric needs you may include whole grain cereal, bread, waffles. (no high fructose corn syrup), yoghurt, nut butters.

BREAKFAST GREEN SHAKE
~ SUPER IMMUNITY SECRETS ~
TIME: 10 minutes

Place in blender:
- 1 c rice, soy or nut milk (almond and hazelnut are excellent)
- 1 heaping T green powder (may contain wheatgrass/barleygrass powder/chlorella/spirulina, and other blends)
- ¼ c unsweetened, shredded raw coconut
- 1 T ground golden flaxseed
- 1 T hemp seed
- 1 banana frozen (broken into pieces before freezing) or other frozen or fresh fruit
- 1-2 pitted dates for sweetness if needed
- 2 tsp rice, soy or whey protein powder (optional)

Blend thoroughly, serve, enjoy.

GREEN POWDER A number of excellent blended green powders can be found online and at your local natural foods grocery that contain algae, dried grasses, herbs, seaweed and juices of plants and vegetables.

Find one you like that fits your budget – and make a green shake daily with it. This type of shake is commonly known as a *SMOOTHIE*. When homemade (without being loaded down with sugar-syrup) this is one of the most light, delicious, easy to digest and nourishing, energizing, regenerative meals. Filled with whole food nutrition it's an excellent replacement for processed whey or soy powders.

Experiment with adding other whole superfoods such as gogi berries and cacao. Filled with healthy nutrition, whole natural foods will help promote healthy leanness manage appetite and provide excellent food value with concentrated quality nutrition.

Chapter 4: Important Things for You
SHOPPING LIST

Here's a list of main ingredients to have on hand. PRINT IT OUT, take to store as checklist. Keep in kitchen and circle what you need. Remember always be creative and add other natural foods you discover to be tasty and nutritious.

VEGGIES (organic best)

Onions
Garlic
Ginger Root
Cilantro
Parsley
Tomatoes
Green Onion
Winter Squash
Peppers
Green Cabbage
Broccoli

Potatoes
Carrots
Spinach
Corn on the Cob
Parsnip
Lemons/Limes
Kale
Avocado
Yams
Sweet Potatoes

FRUIT - all kinds in season

HERBS (buy bulk)
Basil (best fresh)
Dill Weed
Oregano
Rosemary
Thyme

SPICES
Cinnamon
Cumin
Green Chili
Crushed Red Chili

Coriander
Curry blend
Red Chili Powder

NUTRITIOUS ADDITIONS
Cold Pressed Virgin Olive Oil
Coconut Oil (Sunfood link at my site)
Toasted Sesame Oil
Earth or Sea Salt – many available
Miso – try all kinds (nat. food store)
Soy Sauce – natural variety Nama Shoyu Raw
Soy Sauce (opt)
Plain Almond, Hazelnut or Soy Milk

FROZEN
Green Chilies
Peas

Mixed Veggies
French Cut Green Beans

ORIENTAL /HEALTH FOOD
Umeboshi Plum Vinegar
Ume Plums whole or paste (opt)
Rice Noodles
Mung Bean Threads
Toasted Sesame Oil
Soy Sauce, Nama Shoyu (raw)

DAIRY SUBSTITUTES
Rice Cheese – cheddar, mozzarella
Soy Cheese
Soy Sour Cream

DAIRY (Organic)
Plain Yogurt   Sour Cream
Grated Cheeses: cheddar, parmesan, Italian blend

GRAINS
Flour – whole wheat, oat, spelt, rice
Pearled Barley (whole grain pref)
Brown Rice (quick cooking is ok)

BEANS
Pinto   Black
Lentils   Garbanzo
Split Peas (green, yellow, orange, black)
Great Northern

PASTA
Angel Hair
Bowties or other small shapes
Rice Noodles
Rigatoni or Penne Rigate
Ramen Soup or Noodles (msg free)

CANNED *Get fresh when possible, but a few cans make winter and quick food prep easy.*
Diced Tomatoes
Pinto Beans (Mexican seasoned beans)
Black Beans   Garbanzos
Great Northern Beans

Need encouragement?

☑ **TIRED OF STRUGGLING WITH THOSE EXTRA POUNDS?**

☑ **WONDERING WHERE YOUR ENERGY GOT UP AND WENT?**

☑ **IN REMISSION FROM CANCER, HEART DISEASE OR ANOTHER SERIOUS ILLNESS?**

Let CARY Be Your COACH - Get REAL Personal Support -

•Empower yourself to take action now!
•Meet wonderful friends along the way!
•Beat the odds by living a healthy preventive lifestyle now!
•Be one of those who walk versus the many who talk!

Look back one day and be glad you did (for less than a nice dinner out) become part of *Cary's Team* of inspired, health-conscious individuals. Look for details at http://www.caryellis.com

**Access Exclusive
audio/video course
Super Immunity Secrets Lifestyle**

CHANGE YOUR LIFE FOR THE
BETTER NOW.
Every Day You Wait May
Compromise Your Health Later!

Learn Cary's Quick, Easy to Integrate
Everyday Tips and Secrets, Developed over Thirty Years of Working
with World's Top Health Experts.
SPEED LEARNING: Formulated for You in a Speed Learning Format - access
in minutes per day on your cell phone or other mobile device!

**Get Instant Access to Amazing Health Secrets!
You Will Not This Information Together in One Place in One
Easy to Integrate Format Anywhere Else on the Planet.**

SOCIAL NETWORKS – join me!

CLICK HERE TO:

- ✓ FOLLOW ME ON twitter
  http://twitter.com/caryellis

- ✓ BE MY FRIEND ON FACEBOOK:
  http://www.facebook.com/gethealthy

- ✓ SUBSCRIBE / COMMENT You Tube
  http://youtube.com/CaryEllisLifestyle
  http://youtube.com/caryellis489

- ✓ I REPLY REGULARLY
  TO YOUR
  COMMENTS
  ON MY BLOG
  http://
  www.caryellis.com

POWERFUL SECRETS OF REJUVENATION AND VITALITY

If you're serious about being:
- ✓ Healthy
- ✓ Vibrant
- ✓ Energetic
- ✓ Attractive
- ✓ Lean
- ✓ Fit
- ✓ Youthful

The body's *only desire* is to move towards LIFE.

All we have to do is *seriously get out of the way*!

BEGIN Your Journey to Health NOW

IT'S NEVER TOO EARLY OR TOO LATE!

~ you've come to the right place ~

Coming soon at
www.caryellis.com

"If this isn't just idle curiosity and you're serious, then I'm serious about helping you achieve your goal, to guide you every step of the way. If there's something you don't understand or are struggling with, I'm here to assist with support, encouragement and tools for the journey..."

CARY ELLIS

Appendix:
Reference Studies on Super Immunity Ingredients

Chili Pepper

Ahuja KD, Ball MJ. Effects of daily ingestion of chilli on serum lipoprotein oxidation in adult men and women. Br J Nutr. 2006 Aug;96(2): 239-42. 2006. PMID:16923216.

Ahuja KD, Robertson IK, Geraghty DP, Ball MJ. Effects of chili consumption on postprandial glucose, insulin, and energy metabolism. Am J Clin Nutr. 2006 Jul;84(1):63-9. 2006. PMID:16825682.

Attal N. Chronic neuropathic pain: mechanisms and treatment. Clin J Pain 2000 Sep;16(3 Suppl):S118-30 2000.

Ellis CN, Berberian B, et al. A double-blind evaluation of topical capsaicin in pruritic psoriasis. J Amer Acad Dermatol 29:438-42 1993 1993.

Ensminger AH, Esminger M. K. J. e. al. Food for Health: A Nutrition Encyclopedia. Clovis, California: Pegus Press; 1986 1986. PMID: 15210.

Joe B, Lokesh BR. Prophyloatcitc and therapeutic effects of n-3 polyunsaturated fatty acids, capsaicin and curcumin on adjuvant induced arthritis in rats. Nutr Biochem 1997;8:397-407 1997.

Kempaiah RK, Srinivasan K. Integrity of erythrocytes of hypercholesterolemic rats during spices treatment. Mol Cell Biochem 2002 Jul;236(1-2):155-61 2002.

Mori A, Lehmann S, O'Kelly J, Kumagai T, Desmond J, Pervan M, McBride W, Kizaki M, Koeffler HP. Capsaicin, a Component of Red Peppers, Inhibits the Growth of Androgen-Independent, p53 Mutant Prostate Cancer Cells. Cancer Res 2006 Mar 15;66(6):3222-9. 2006. PMID:16540674.

Rains C, Bryson HM. Topical capsaicin. A review of its pharmacological properties and therapeutic potential in post-herpetic neuralgia, diabetic neuropathy and osteoarthritis. Drugs Aging 1995 Oct;7(4): 317-28 1995.

Robbins W. Clinical applications of capsaicinoids. Clin J Pain 2000 Jun;16(2 Suppl):S86-9 2000.

Schnitzer TJ. Non-NSAID pharmacologic treatment options for the management of chronic pain. Am J Med 1998 Jul 27;105(1B):45S-52S 1998.

Wood, Rebecca. The Whole Foods Encyclopedia. New York, NY: Prentice-Hall Press; 1988 1988. PMID:15220.

Cilantro/Coriander

Ballal RS, Jacobsen DW, Robinson K. Homocysteine: update on a new risk factor. Cleve Clin J Med 1997 Nov-1997 Dec 31;64(10):543-9 1997.

Chithra V, Leelamma S. Hypolipidemic effect of coriander seeds (Coriandrum sativum): mechanism of action. Plant Foods Hum Nutr 1997;51(2):167-72 1997. PMID: 12610.

Chithra V, Leelamma S. Coriandrum sativum changes the levels of lipid peroxides and activity of antioxidant enzymes in experimental animals. Indian J Biochem Biophys 1999 Feb;36(1):59-61 1999. PMID:12590.

Delaquis PJ, Stanich K, Girard B et al. Antimicrobial activity of individual and mixed fractions of dill, cilantro, coriander and eucalyptus essential oils. Int J Food Microbiol. 2002 Mar 25;74(1-2):101-9 2002.

Ensminger AH, Esminger M. K. J. e. al. Food for Health: A Nutrition Encyclopedia. Clovis, California: Pegus Press; 1986 1986. PMID:15210.

Fortin, Francois, Editorial Director. The Visual Foods Encyclopedia. Macmillan, New York 1996.

Gray AM, Flatt PR. Insulin-releasing and insulin-like activity of the traditional anti-diabetic plant Coriandrum sativum (coriander). Br J Nutr 1999 Mar;81(3): 203-9 1999. PMID:12600.

Grieve M. A Modern Herbal. Dover Publications, New York 1971.

Kubo I, Fujita K, Kubo A, Nihei K, Ogura T. Antibacterial Activity of Coriander Volatile Compounds against Salmonella choleraesuis. J Agric Food Chem. 2004 Jun 2;52(11): 3329-32. 2004. PMID:15161192.

Wood, Rebecca. The Whole Foods Encyclopedia. New York, NY: Prentice-Hall Press; 1988. PMID:15220.

Dill

Ensminger AH, Esminger M. K. J. e. al. Food for Health: A Nutrition Encyclopedia. Clovis, California: Pegus Press; 1986 1986. PMID: 15210.

Fortin, Francois, Editorial Director. The Visual Foods Encyclopedia. Macmillan, NY 1996.

Grieve M. A Modern Herbal. Dover Publications, New York 1971.

Singh G, Kapoor IP, Pandey SK et al. Studies on essential oils: part 10; antibacterial activity of volatile oils of some spices. Phytother Res 2002 Nov;16(7):680-2 2002.

Wood, Rebecca. The Whole Foods Encyclopedia. New York, NY: Prentice-Hall Press; 1988 1988. PMID:15220.

Zheng GQ, Kenney PM, Lam LK. Anethofuran, carvone, and limonene: potential cancer chemopreventive agents from dill weed oil and caraway oil. Planta Med 1992 Aug;58(4): 338-41 1992. PMID:12200.

Miso

Baggott JE, et al. Effect of Miso (Japanese Soybean Paste) and NaCl on DMBA-Induced Rat Mammary Tumors. Nutrition and Cancer 14:103-09, 1990 1990.

Ensminger AH, Esminger M. K. J. e. al. Food for Health: A Nutrition Encyclopedia. Clovis, California: Pegus Press; 1986 1986. PMID: 15210.

Fortin, Francois, Editorial Director. The Visual Foods Encyclopedia. Macmillan, NY 1996.

Wood, Rebecca. The Whole Foods Encyclopedia. New York, NY: Prentice-Hall Press; 1988 1988. PMID:15220.

Garlic

Adlercreutz H. Western diet and Western diseases: some hormonal and biochemical mechanisms and associations. Scand J Clin Lab Invest. 1990:50(S201):3-23 1990.

American Botanical Council. New Research Supports Garlic's Role in Arresting and Reversing Arteriosclerosis. www. Herbalgram.org, the e-newsletter of the Amer. Botanical Council, April 29, 2005. 2005.

Andorfer JH, Tchaikovskaya T, Listowsky I. Selective expression of glutathione S-transferase genes in the murine gastrointestinal tract in response to dietary organosulfur compounds. Carcinogenesis 2003 Nov 21 [Epub ahead of print]. 2003.

Anwar MM, Meki AR. Oxidative stress in streptozotocin-induced diabetic rats: effects of garlic oil and melatonin. Comp Biochem Physiol A Mol Integr Physiol. Aug;135(4): 539-547 2003.

Baluchnejadmojarad T, Roghani M. Endothelium-dependent and -independent effect of aqueous extract of garlic on vascular reactivity on diabetic rats. Fitoterapia. 2003 Dec;74(7-8):630-7.'03.

Bautista DM, Movahed P, Hinman A, Axelsson HE, Sterner O, HOgestatt ED, Julius D, Jordt SE, Zygmunt PM. Pungent products from garlic activate the sensory ion channel TRPA1. Proc Natl Acad Sci U S A. 2005 Aug 15; [Epub ahead of print] 2005. PMID:16103371.

Bhattacharya K, Yadava S, Papp T, Schiffmann D, Rahman Q. Reduction of chrysotile asbestos-induced genotoxicity in human peripheral blood lymphocytes by garlic extract. Toxicol Lett. 2004 Nov 28;153(3):327-32. 2004. PMID:15454308.

Cavagnaro PF, Camargo A, Galmarini CR, Simon PW. Effect of cooking on garlic (Allium sativum L.) antiplatelet activity and thiosulfinates content. J Agric Food Chem. 2007 Feb 21;55(4):1280-8. Epub 2007 Jan 27. 2007. PMID:17256959.

Durak I, Aytac B, Atmaca Y, Devrim E, Avci A, Erol C, Oral D. Effects of garlic extract consumption on plasma and erythrocyte antioxidant parameters in atherosclerotic patients. Life Sci. 2004 Sep 3;75(16): 1959-66. 2004. PMID:15306163.

Elkayam A, Mirelman D, Peleg E, Wilchek M, Miron T, Rabinkov A, Oron-Herman M, Rosenthal T. The effects of allicin on weight in fructose-induced hyperinsulinemic, hyperlipidemic, hypertensive rats. Am J Hypertens. 2003 Dec; 16(12):1053-6. 2003.

Galeone C, Pelucchi C, Levi F, Negri E, Franceschi S, Talamini R, Giacosa A, La Vecchia C. Onion and garlic use and human cancer. Am J Clin Nutr. 2006 Nov;84(5):1027-32. 2006. PMID: 17093154.

Keiss HP, Dirsch VM, Hartung T, Haffner T, Trueman L, Auger J, Kahane R, Vollmar AM. Garlic (Allium sativum L.) modulates cytokine expression in lipopolysaccharide-activated human blood thereby inhibiting NF-kappaB activity. J Nutr. Jul;133(7):2171-5. 2003.

Lee YL, Cesario T, Wang Y, Shanbrom E, Thrupp L. Antibacterial activity of vegetables and juices. Nutrition. 2003 Nov-Dec;19(11-12):994-6. 2003.

Salih BA, Abasiyanik FM. Does regular garlic intake affect the prevalence of Helicobacter pylori in asymptomatic subjects. Saudi Med J. Aug;24(8):842-5. 2003.

Siegel G, Michel F, Ploch M, Rodriguez M, Malmsten M. [Inhibition of arteriosclerotic plaque development by garlic]. Wien Med Wochenschr. 2004 Nov;154(21-22):515-22. 2004. PMID:15638070.

Tapsell LC, Hemphill I, Cobiac L, Patch CS, Sullivan DR, Fenech M, Roodenrys S, Keogh JB, Clifton PM, Williams PG, Fazio VA, Inge KE. Health benefits of herbs and spices: the past, the present, the future. Med J Aust. 2006 Aug 21;185(4 Suppl):S4-24. 2006. PMID: 17022438.

Tilli CM, Stavast-Kooy AJ, Vuerstaek JD, Thissen MR, Krekels GA, Ramaekers FC, Neumann HA. The garlic-derived organosulfur component ajoene decreases basal cell carcinoma tumor size by inducing apoptosis. Arch Dermatol Res. Jul;295(3):117-23. 2003.

Tsao SM, Hsu CC, Yin MC. Garlic extract and two diallyl sulphides inhibit methicillin-resistant Staphylococcus aureus infection in BALB/cA mice. J Antimicrob Chemother. 2003 Dec; 52(6):974-80. 2003.

Wilson CL, Aboyade-Cole A, Darling-Reed S, Thomas RD. Poster Presentations, Session A, Abstract 2543: A30 Diallyl Sulfide Antagonizes PhIP Induced Alterations in the Expression of Phase I and Phase II Metabolizing Enzymes in Human Breast Epithelial Cells. presented at the Amer. Assoc. for Cancer Research's Frontiers in Cancer Prevention Research meeting in Baltimore, MD, July 2005. 2005.

Ginger

Akoachere JF, Ndip RN, Chenwi EB et al. Antibacterial effect of Zingiber officinale and Garcinia kola on respiratory tract pathogens. East Afr Med J. 2002 Nov;79(11):588-92 2002.

Bode A. Ginger is an effective inhibitor of HCT116 human colorectal carcinoma in vivo. paper presented at the Frontiers in Cancer Prevention Research Conference, Phoenix, AZ, Ocbober 26-3-, 2003 2003.

Borrelli F, Capasso R, Aviello G, Pittler MH, Izzo AA. Effectiveness and safety of ginger in the treatment of pregnancy-induced nausea and vomiting. Obstet Gynecol. 2005 Apr;105(4): 849-56. 2005. PMID:15802416.

Ensminger AH, Ensminger, ME, Kondale JE, Robson JRK. Foods & Nutriton Encyclopedia. Pegus Press, Clovis, California 1983.

Ensminger AH, Esminger M. K. J. e. al. Food for Health: A Nutrition Encyclopedia. Clovis, California: Pegus Press; 1986 1986. PMID: 15210.

Ficker CE, Arnason JT, Vindas PS et al. Inhibition of human pathogenic fungi by ethnobotanically selected plant extracts. Mycoses. 2003 Feb;46(1-2):29-37 2003.

Fischer-Rasmussen W, Kjaer SK, Dahl C, et al. Ginger treatment of hypereesis gravidarum. Eur J Obstet Gynecol Reprod Biol 38(1990): 19-24 1990.

Fortin, Francois, Editorial Director. The Visual Foods Encyclopedia. Macmillan, New York 1996.

Grieve M. A Modern Herbal. Dover Publications, New York 1971.

Ippoushi K, Azuma K, Ito H, Horie H, Higashio H. [6]-Gingerol inhibits nitric oxide in activated J774.1 mouse macrophages, prevents peroxynitrite induced oxidation and nitration reactions. Life Sci. 2003 Nov 14;73(26): 3427-37. 2003.

Jagetia GC, Baliga MS, Venkatesh P, Ulloor JN. Influence of ginger rhizome (Zingiber officinale Rosc) on survival, glutathione and lipid peroxidation in mice after whole-body exposure to gamma radiation. Radiat Res. 2003 Nov;160(5):584-92. 2003.

Kiuchi F, et al. Inhibition of prostaglandin and leukotriene biosynthesis by gingerols and diarylheptanoids. Chem Pharm Bull 40 (1992): 387-91 1992.

Nature Immunology Online. Nature Immunology Online. 2001;10.1038/ni732 2001.

Phan PV, Sohrabi A, Polotsky A, Hungerford DS, Lindmark L, Frondoza CG. Ginger extract components suppress induction of chemokine expression in human synoviocytes. J Altern Complement Med. 2005 Feb;11(1):149-54. 2005. PMID:15750374.

Rhode JM, Huang J, Fogoros S, Tan L, Zick S, Liu JR. Ginger induces apoptosis and autophagocytosis in ovarian cancer cells. Abstract #4510, presented April 4, 2006 at the 97th AACR Annual Meeting, April 1-5, 2006, Washington, DC. 2006.

Srivastava KC, Mustafa T. Ginger (Zingiber officinale) in rheumatism and musculoskeletal disorders. Med Hypothesis 39(1992):342-8 1992.

Srivastava KC, Mustafa T. Ginger (Zingiber officinale) and rheumatic disorders. Med Hypothesis 29 (1989):25-28 1989.

Wigler I, Grotto I, Caspi D, Yaron M. The effects of Zintona EC (a ginger extract) on symptomatic gonarthritis. Osteoarthritis Cartilage. 2003 Nov;11(11):783-9. 2003.

Wood, Rebecca. The Whole Foods Encyclopedia. New York, NY: Prentice-Hall Press; 1988 1988. PMID:15220.

Olive Oil, extra virgin

Aguilera CM, Ramirez-Tortosa MC, Mesa MD, Gil A. [Protective effect of monounsaturated and polyunsaturated fatty acids on the development of cardiovascular disease]. Nutr Hosp 2001 May-2001 Jun 30;16(3):78-91 2001. PMID:11620.

Alarcon de la Lastra C, Barranco MD, Motilva V, Herrerias JM. Mediterranean diet and health: biological importance of olive oil. Curr Pharm Des. 2001 Jul;7(10):933-50. 2001. PMID: 11472248.

Beauchamp GK, Keast RS, Morel D, Lin J, Pika J, Han Q, Lee CH, Smith AB, Breslin PA. Phytochemistry: ibuprofen-like activity in extra-virgin olive oil. Nature. 2005 Sep 1;437(7055):45-6. 2005. PMID:16136122.

Bond R, Lloyd DH. A double-blind comparison of olive oil and a combination of evening primrose oil and fish oil in the management of canine atopy. Vet Rec 1992 Dec 12;131(24): 558-60 1992. PMID:11330.

Bondia-Pons I, Schroder H, Covas MI, Castellote AI, Kaikkonen J, Poulsen HE, Gaddi AV, Machowetz A, Kiesewetter H, Lopez-Sabater MC. Moderate consumption of olive oil by healthy European men reduces systolic blood pressure in non-Mediterranean participants. J Nutr. 2007 Jan;137(1):84-87. 2007. PMID: 17182805.

Caponio F, Bilancia MT, Pasqualone A, Sikorska E, Gomes T. Influence of the exposure to light on extra virgin olive oil quality during storage. European Food Research and Technology, 2005 July; 221(1-2):92-98. 2005.

Carluccio MA, Siculella L, Ancora MA et al. Olive oil and red wine antioxidant polyphenols inhibit endothelial activation antiatherogenic properties of mediterranean diet phytochemicals. Arterioscler Thromb Vasc Biol 2003 Apr 1; 23(4):622-9 2003.

Covas MI, de la Torre K, Farre-Albaladejo M, Kaikkonen J, Fito M, Lopez-Sabater C, Pujadas-Bastardes MA, Joglar J, Weinbrenner T, Lamuela-Raventos RM, de la Torre R. Postprandial LDL phenolic content and LDL oxidation are modulated by olive oil phenolic compounds in humans. Free Radic Biol Med. 2006 Feb 15;40(4):608-16. Epub 2005 Oct 18. 2006. PMID:16458191.

Covas MI, Nyyssonen K, Poulsen HE, Kaikkonen J, Zunft HJ, Kiesewetter H, Gaddi A, de la Torre R, Mursu J, Baumler H, Nascetti S, Salonen JT, Fito M, Virtanen J, Marrugat J. EUROLIVE Study Group. The effect of polyphenols in olive oil on heart disease risk factors: a randomized trial. Ann Intern Med. 2006 Sep 5;145(5):333-41. 2006. PMID:16954359.

Covas MI. Olive oil and the cardiovascular system. Pharmacol Res. 2007 Mar;55(3):175-86. Epub 2007 Jan 30. 2007. PMID:17321749.

Ensminger AH, Esminger M. K. J. e. al. Food for Health: A Nutrition Encyclopedia. Clovis, California: Pegus Press; 1986 1986. PMID: 15210.

Garcia-Segovia P, Sanchez-Villegas A, Doreste J, Santana F, Serra-Majem L. Olive oil consumption and risk of breast cancer in the Canary Islands: a population-based case-control study. Public Health Nutr 2006 Feb; 9(1A):163-7. 2006. PMID:16512965.

Gill CI, Boyd A, McDermott E, McCann M, Servili M, Selvaggini R, Taticchi A, Esposto S, Montedoro G, McGlynn H, Rowland I. Potential anti-cancer effects of virgin olive oil phenols on colorectal carcinogenesis models *in vitro*. Int J Cancer. 2005 Oct 20;117(1):1-7. 2005. PMID:15880398.

Haban P, Klvanova J, Zidekova E, Nagyova A. Dietary supplementation with olive oil leads to improved lipoprotein spectrum and lower n-6 PUFAs in elderly subjects. Dietary supplementation with olive oil leads to improved lipoprotein spectrum and lower n-6 PUFAs in elderly subjects. Med Sci Monit. 2004 Mar 23;10(4):PI49-PI54. 2004. PMID:15039655.

Hashim YZ, Eng M, Gill CI, McGlynn H, Rowland IR. Components of olive oil and chemoprevention of colorectal cancer. Nutr Rev. 2005 Nov;63(11):374-86. 2005. PMID: 16370222.

Hillestrom PR, Covas MI, Poulsen HE. Effect of dietary virgin olive oil on urinary excretion of etheno-DNA adducts. Free Radic Biol Med. 2006 Oct 1;41(7):1133-8. Epub 2006 Jul 4. 2006. PMID:16962938.

Kontogianni MD, Panagiotakos DB, Chrysohoou C, Pitsavos C, Zampelas A, Stefanadis C. The impact of olive oil consumption pattern on the risk of acute coronary syndromes: The CARDIO2000 case-control study. Clin Cardiol. 2007 Mar;30(3):125-9. 2007. PMID:17385704.

Machowetz A, Poulsen HE, Gruendel S, Weimann A, Fito M, Marrugat J, de la Torre R, Salonen JT, Nyyssonen K, Mursu J, Nascetti S, Gaddi A, Kiesewetter H, Baumler H, Selmi H, Kaikkonen J, Zunft HJ, Cova. Effect of olive oils on biomarkers of oxidative DNA stress in Northern and Southern Europeans. FASEB J. 2007 Jan;21(1):45-52. Epub 2006 Nov 16. 2007. PMID:17110467

Marrugat J, Covas MI, Fito M, Schroder H, Miro-Casas E, Gimeno E, Lopez-Sabater MC, De La Torre R, Farre M. Effects of differing phenolic content in dietary olive oils on lipids and LDL oxidation: A randomized controlled trial. Eur J Nutr. 2004 Jun;43(3):140-7. 2004. PMID: 15168036.

Martinez-Dominguez E, de la Puerta R, Ruiz-Gutierrez V. Protective effects upon experimental inflammation models of a polyphenol-supplemented virgin olive oil diet. Inflamm Res 2001 Feb;50(2):102-6 2001. PMID:11630.

Masella R, Vari R, D'Archivio M, Di Benedetto R, Matarrese P, Malorni W, Scazzocchio B, Giovannini C. Extra Virgin Olive Oil Biophenols Inhibit Cell-Mediated Oxidation of LDL by Increasing the mRNA Transcription of Glutathione-Related Enzymes. J Nutr. 2004 Apr;134(4):785-91. 2004. PMID:15051826.

Masia R, Pena A, Marrugat J, Sala J, Vila J, Pavesi M, Covas M, Aubo C, Elosua R. High prevalence of cardiovascular risk factors in Gerona, Spain, a province with low myocardial infarction incidence. REGICOR Investigators. J Epidemiol Community Health. 1998 Nov;52(11):707-15. 1998. PMID: 10396503.

Menendez JA, Vellon L, Colomer R, Lupu R. Oleic acid, the main monounsaturated fatty acid of olive oil, suppresses Her-2/neu (erbB-2) expression and synergistically enhances the growth inhibitory effects of trastuzumab (HerceptinTM) in breast. Ann Oncol. 2005 Jan 10; [Epub ahead of print] 2005. PMID: 15642702.

Morello JR, Motilva MJ, Tovar MJ, Romero MP. Changes in commercial virgin olive oil (cv Arbequina) during storage, with special emphasis on phenolic fraction. J Agric Food Chem, 2004 May; 85(3):357-364. 2004.

Moreno DA, López-Berenguer C, García-Viguera C. Effects of stir-fry cooking with different edible oils on the phytochemical composition of broccoli. J Food Sci. 2007 Jan; 72(1):S064-8. 2007. PMID:17995900.

Moreno JJ. Effect of olive oil minor components on oxidative stress and arachidonic acid mobilization and metabolism by macrophages RAW 264.7. Free Radic Biol Med. 2003 Nov 1;35(9):1073-81. 2003.

Paniagua JA, Gallego de la Sacristana A, Romero I, Vidal-Puig A, Latre JM, Sanchez E, Perez-Martinez P, Lopez-Miranda J, Perez-Jimenez F. Monounsaturated fat-rich diet prevents central body fat distribution and decreases postprandial adiponectin expression induced by a carbohydrate-rich diet in insulin-resistant subjects. Diabetes Care. 2007 Jul;30(7): 1717-23. Epub 2007 Mar 23. 2007. PMID: 17384344.

Persson E, Graziani G, Ferracane R, Fogliano V, Skog K. Influence of antioxidants in virgin olive oil on the formation of heterocyclic amines in fried beefburgers. Food Chem Toxicol. 2003 Nov;41(11):1587-97. 2003.

Piers LS, Walker KZ, Stoney RM, Soares MJ, O'Dea K. Substitution of saturated with monounsaturated fat in a 4-week diet affects body weight and composition of overweight and obese men. Br J Nutr. 2003 Sep;90(3): 717-27 2003.

Psaltopoulou T, Naska A, Orfanos P, Trichopoulos D, Mountokalakis T, Trichopoulou A. Olive oil, the Mediterranean diet, and arterial blood pressure: the Greek European Prospective Investigation into Cancer and Nutrition (EPIC) study. Am J Clin Nutr. 2004 Oct;80(4):1012-8. 2004. PMID:15447913.

Puel C, Mathey J, Agalias A, Kati-Coulibaly S, Mardon J, Obled C, Davicco MJ, Lebecque P, Horcajada MN, Skaltsounis AL, Coxam V. Dose-response study of effect of oleuropein, an olive oil polyphenol, in an ovariectomy/ inflammation experimental model of bone loss in the rat. Clin Nutr. 2006 May 30; [Epub ahead of print] 2006. PMID:16740345.

Puel C, Quintin A, Agalias A, Mathey J, Obled C, Mazur A, Davicco MJ, Lebecque P, Skaltsounis AL, Coxam V. Olive oil and its main phenolic micronutrient (oleuropein) prevent inflammation-induced bone loss in the ovariectomised rat. Br J Nutr. 2004 Jul;92(1): 119-27. 2004. PMID:15230995.

Romero C, Medina E, Vargas J, Brenes M, Castro AD. In Vitro Activity of Olive Oil Polyphenols against Helicobacter pylori. J Agric Food Chem. 2007 Feb 7;55(3):680-6. 2007. PMID: 17263460.

Ruano J, López-Miranda J, de la Torre R, Delgado-Lista J, Fernández J, Caballero J, Covas MI, Jiménez Y, Pérez-Martínez P, Marín C, Fuentes F, Pérez-Jiménez F. Intake of phenol-rich virgin olive oil improves the postprandial prothrombotic profile in hypercholesterolemic patients. Am J Clin Nutr. 2007 Aug;86(2): 341-6. 2007. PMID:17684203.

Ruano J, Lopez-Miranda J, Fuentes F, Moreno JA, Bellido C, Perez-Martinez P, Lozano A, Gomez P, Jimenez Y, Perez Jimenez F. Phenolic content of virgin olive oil improves ischemic reactive hyperemia in hypercholesterolemic patients. J Am Coll Cardiol. 2005 Nov 15;46(10):1864-8. 2005. PMID:16286173.

Salvini S, Sera F, Caruso D, Giovannelli L, Visioli F, Saieva C, Masala G, Ceroti M, Giovacchini V, Pitozzi V, Galli C, Romani A, Mulinacci N, Bortolomeazzi R, Dolara P, Palli D. Daily consumption of a high-phenol extra-virgin olive oil reduces oxidative DNA damage in postmenopausal women. Br J Nutr. 2006 Apr; 95(4):742-51. 2006. PMID:16571154.

Soriguer F, Moreno F, Rojo-Martinez G, Garcia-Fuentes E, Tinahones F, Gomez-Zumaquero JM, Cuesta-Munoz AL, Cardona F, Morcillo S. Monounsaturated n-9 fatty acids and adipocyte lipolysis in rats.Br J Nutr. 2003 Dec; 90(6):1015-22. 2003.

Valavanidis A, Nisiotou C, Papageorgiou Y, Kremli I, Satravelas N, Zinieris N, Zygalaki H. Comparison of the Radical Scavenging Potential of Polar and Lipidic Fractions of Olive Oil and Other Vegetable Oils under Normal Conditions and after Thermal Treatment.J Agric Food Chem. 2004 Apr 21;52(8): 2358-65. 2004. PMID:15080646.

Visioli F, Romani A, Mulinacci N, et al. Antioxidant and other biological activities of olive mill waste waters. J Agric Food Chem 1999 Aug; 47(8):3397-401 1999. PMID:11320.

Onion

Ali M, Thomson M, Afzal M. Garlic and onions: their effect on eicosanoid metabolism and its clinical relevance. Prostaglandins Leukot Essent Fatty Acids. 2000 Feb;62(2):55-73. Review 2000.

Augusti KT. Therapeutic values of onion (Allium cepa L.) and garlic (Allium sativum L.). Indian J Exp Biol. 1996 Jul;34(7):634-40. Rev. 1996.

Challier B, Perarnau JM, Viel JF. Garlic, onion and cereal fibre as protective factors for breast cancer: a French case-control study. Eur J Epidemiol 1998 Dec;14(8):737-47 1998. PMID:13640.

Cruz-Correa M, Shoskes DA, Sanchez P, Zhao R, Hylind LM, Wexner SD, Giardiello FM. Combination treatment with curcumin and quercetin of adenomas in familial adenomatous polyposis. i>Clin Gastroenterol Hepatol. 2006 Aug;4(8):1035-8. Epub 2006 Jun 6. 2006. PMID:16757216.

Dorant E, van den Brandt PA, Goldbohm RA. A prospective cohort study on the relationship between onion and leek consumption, garlic supplement use and the risk of colorectal carcinoma in The Netherlands. Carcinogenesis 1996 Mar;17(3):477-84 1996. PMID:13660.

Dorsch W, Ettl M, Hein G, et al. Antiasthmatic effects of onions. Inhibition of platelet-activating factor-induced bronchial obstruction by onion oils. Int Arch Allergy Appl Immunol. 1987;82(3-4):535-6 1987.

Ensminger AH, Ensminger, ME, Kondale JE, Robson JRK. Foods & Nutriton Encyclopedia. Pegus Press, Clovis, California 1983.

Ensminger AH, Esminger M. K. J. e. al. Food for Health: A Nutrition Encyclopedia. Clovis, California: Pegus Press; 1986 1986. PMID: 15210.

Fortin, Francois, Editorial Director. The Visual Foods Encyclopedia. Macmillan, New York 1996.

Fukushima S, Takada N, Hori T, Wanibuchi H. Cancer prevention by organosulfur compounds from garlic and onion. J Cell Biochem Suppl 1997;27:100-5 1997. PMID: 13650.

Galeone C, Pelucchi C, Levi F, Negri E, Franceschi S, Talamini R, Giacosa A, La Vecchia C. Onion and garlic use and human cancer. Am J Clin Nutr. 2006 Nov;84(5):1027-32. 2006. PMID: 17093154.

Gates MA, Tworoger SS, Hecht JL, De Vivo I, Rosner B, Hankinson SE. A prospective study of dietary flavonoid intake and incidence of epithelial ovarian cancer. Int J Cancer. 2007 Apr 30; [Epub ahead of print] 2007. PMID: 17471564.

Gee JM, Hara HT. Suppression of Intestinal Crypt Cell Proliferation and Aberrant Crypt Foci by Dietary Quercetin in Rats. Nutr Cancer 2002;43(2):121-126 2002.

Grieve M. A Modern Herbal. Dover Publications, New York 1971.

Huxley RR, Neil HAW. The relation between dietary flavonol intake and coronary heart disease mortality: a meta-analysis of prospective cohort studies,. European Journal of Clinical Nutrition (2003) 57, 904-908. 2003.

Manach C, Scalbert A, Morand C, Rémésy C, Jiménez L. Polyphenols: food sources and bioavailability. Am J Clin Nutr. 2004 May; 79(5):727-47. 2004. PMID:15113710.

Moon JH, Nakata R, Oshima S, et al. Accumulation of quercetin conjugates in blood plasma after the short-term ingestion of onion by women. Am J Physiol Regul Integr Comp Physiol. 2000 Aug; 279(2):R461-7 2000.

Riley DM, Bianchini F, Vainio H. Allium vegetables and organosulfur compounds: do they help prevent cancer. Environ Health Perspect 2001 Sep;109(9):893-902 2001. PMID:13600.

Sheela CG, Kumud K, Augusti KT. Anti-diabetic effects of onion and garlic sulfoxide amino acids in rats. Planta Med. 1995 Aug;61(4): 356-7 1995.

Vanderhoek J, Makheja A, Bailey J. Inhibition of fatty acid lipoxygenases by onion and garlic oils: Evidence for the mechanism by which these oils inhibit platelet aggregation. Bioch Pharmacol 29 (1980):3169-73 1980.

Wagner H, Dorsch W, Bayer T, et al. Antiasthmatic effects of onions: inhibition of 5-lipoxygenase and cyclooxygenase in vitro by thiosulfinates and "Cepaenes". Prostaglandins Leukot Essent Fatty Acids. 1990 Jan;39(1):59-62 1990.

Wetli HA, Brenneisen R, Tschudi I, Langos M, Bigler P, Sprang T, Schurch S, Muhlbauer RC. A gamma-Glutamyl Peptide Isolated from Onion (Allium cepa L.) by Bioassay-Guided Fractionation Inhibits Resorption Activity of Osteoclasts. J Agric Food Chem. 2005 May 4;53(9):3408-3414. 2005. PMID:15853380.

Wood, Rebecca. The Whole Foods Encyclopedia. New York, NY: Prentice-Hall Press; 1988 1988. PMID:15220.

Yang J, Meyers KJ, van der Heide J, Liu RH. Varietal Differences in Phenolic Content and Antioxidant and Antiproliferative Activities of Onions. J Agric Food Chem. 2004 Nov 3;52(22):6787-6793. 2004. PMID:15506817.

Oregano

Akgul A, Kivanc M. Inhibitory effects of selected Turkish spices and oregano components on some foodborne fungi. Int J Food Microbiol 1988 May;6(3):263-8 1988. PMID:12430.

Ensminger AH, Ensminger, ME, Kondale JE, Robson JRK. Foods & Nutriton Encyclopedia. Pegus Press, Clovis, California 1983.

Ensminger AH, Esminger M. K. J. e. al. Food for Health: A Nutrition Encyclopedia. Clovis, California: Pegus Press; 1986 1986. PMID: 15210.

Fortin, Francois, Editorial Director. The Visual Foods Encyclopedia. Macmillan, NY 1996.

Grieve M. A Modern Herbal. Dover Publications, New York 1971.

Lagouri V, Boskou D. Nutrient antioxidants in oregano. Int J Food Sci Nutr 1996 Nov;47(6): 493-7 1996. PMID:12400.

Lambert RJ, Skandamis PN, Coote PJ, Nychas GJ. A study of the minimum inhibitory concentration and mode of action of oregano essential oil, thymol and carvacrol. J Appl Microbiol 2001 Sep;91(3):453-62 2001. PMID:12450.

Martinez-Tome M, Jimenez AM, Ruggieri S, et al. Antioxidant properties of Mediterranean spices compared with common food additives. J Food Prot 2001 Sep;64(9):1412-9 2001. PMID: 12440.

Takacsova M, Pribela A, Faktorova M. Study of the antioxidative effects of thyme, sage, juniper and oregano. Nahrung 1995;39(3):241-3 1995. PMID:12410.

Wood, Rebecca. The Whole Foods Encyclopedia. New York, NY: Prentice-Hall Press; 1988 1988. PMID:15220.

Zheng W, Wang SY. Antioxidant activity and phenolic compounds in selected herbs. J Agric Food Chem 2002;49:5165-70 2002.

Fortin, Francois, Editorial Director. The Visual Foods Encyclopedia. Macmillan, NY1996.

Parsley

Ensminger AH, Ensminger, ME, Kondale JE, Robson JRK. Foods & Nutriton Encyclopedia. Pegus Press, Clovis, California 1983.

Ensminger AH, Esminger M. K. J. e. al. Food for Health: A Nutrition Encyclopedia. Clovis, California: Pegus Press; 1986 1986. PMID: 15210.

Fortin, Francois, Editorial Director. The Visual Foods Encyclopedia. Macmillan, New York 1996.

Grieve M. A Modern Herbal. Dover Publications, New York 1971.

Hirano R, Sasamoto W, Matsumoto A et al. Antioxidant ability of various flavonoids against DPPH radicals and LDL oxidation. J Nutr Sci Vitaminol (Tokyo). 2001 Oct;47(5): 357-62 2001.

Pattison DJ, Silman AJ, Goodson NJ, Lunt M, Bunn D, Luben R, Welch A, Bingham S, Khaw KT, Day N, Symmons DP. Vitamin C and the risk of developing inflammatory polyarthritis: prospective nested case-control study. Ann Rheum Dis. 2004 Jul;63(7):843-7. 2004. PMID:15194581.

Sasaki N, Toda T, Kaneko T et al. Protective effects of flavonoids on the cytotoxicity of linoleic acid hydroperoxide toward rat pheochromocytoma PC12 cells. Chem Biol Interact. 2003 Mar 6;145(1):101-16 2003.

Wood, Rebecca. The Whole Foods Encyclopedia. New York, NY: Prentice-Hall Press; 1988 1988. PMID:15220.

Soy Sauce

Ensminger AH, Esminger M. K. J. e. al. Food for Health: A Nutrition Encyclopedia. Clovis, Calif.: Pegus Press; 1986 1986. PMID:15210.

Fortin, Francois, Editorial Director. The Visual Foods Encyclopedia. Macmillan, NY1996.

Wood, Rebecca. The Whole Foods Encyclopedia. New York, NY: Prentice-Hall Press; 1988 1988. PMID:15220.

Peppermint/Spearmint

Edris AE, Farrag ES. Antifungal activity of peppermint and sweet basil essential oils and their major aroma constituents on some plant pathogenic fungi from the vapor phase. Nahrung 2003 Apr; 47(2):117-21 2003.

Ensminger AH, Ensminger, ME, Kondale JE, Robson JRK. Foods & Nutriton Encyclopedia. Pegus Press, Clovis, California 1983.

Ensminger AH, Esminger M. K. J. e. al. Food for Health: A Nutrition Encyclopedia. Clovis, California: Pegus Press; 1986 1986. PMID: 15210.

Fortin, Francois, Editorial Director. The Visual Foods Encyclopedia. Macmillan, NY 1996.

Grieve M. A Modern Herbal. Dover Publications, New York 1971.

Wood, Rebecca. The Whole Foods Encyclopedia. New York, NY: Prentice-Hall Press; 1988 1988. PMID:15220.

You Got the Book.
Now get the video course.
Make it a Lifestyle.

Learn How to Adopt Diet and Lifestyle shown by Research to help Beat Colds, Flu, Cancer, Heart Disease and serious illness Before they Beat You

http://www.caryellis.com

RESULTS MAY VARY.
SEEK THE ADVICE OF A PHYSICIAN BEFORE ADOPTING ANY DIETARY OR LIFESTYLE CHANGES

17781192R00045

Made in the USA
Middletown, DE
07 February 2015